Early praise for *Remote Pairing*

I'm convinced that remote pair programming is a big part of the future of software development. People are constantly asking me, "How do I get started with remote pairing?" This book is the answer to that question. It's short, sweet, and hits on the important tools and techniques without any extraneous fluff. I particularly like that Joe digs into some less common tech, like the Eclipse plug-in and NX.

➤ **Avdi Grimm**
   Head Chef, RubyTapas.com

This book is *important*. As more and more developers discover the benefits of working remotely, developers and employers alike must be prepared with tools and processes to allow collaboration regardless of physical distance. This short book, more effectively than anything I've seen thus far, dispels the myth that pair programming can't work for distributed teams. It provides a blueprint to doing remote pairing right.

➤ **Ernie Miller**
   Senior Rubyist, Appriss

All distributed teams can benefit from this book. Not only is it an extremely useful guide to the nuts and bolts of remote pair programming, but it also explains why remote pairing, and pair programming in general, is so beneficial.

➤ **Joe Moore**
   Principal Developer, Pivotal Labs

Remote Pairing does a great job of introducing new technologies, but I found Joe's examination of real-world pairing to be particularly valuable. The insight in this book helped me identify why some sessions fail or become frustrating, and it provided me with great advice on making future sessions successful and enjoyable.

➤ **Chad Taylor**
  Developer, deciBel Research, Inc

As a developer who pairs remotely every day, I know of no other source that provides such a variety of information to help developers pair remotely. Even with all of my remote-pairing experience I found some new tools and techniques in *Remote Pairing*.

➤ **Chris Johnson**
  Software Engineer, Getty Images

This book is a well-organized and easy-to-read guide for programmers of all kinds. Joe provides excellent instructions for overcoming common problems associated with working remotely. From screen sharing to IDEs, Joe covers all the tools that made it possible for him and me to work together despite living on opposite sides of the world.

➤ **Vamsi Krishna Jandhyala**
  Java Developer, Pune, India

Remote Pairing

Collaborative Tools for Distributed Development

Joe Kutner

The Pragmatic Bookshelf

Dallas, Texas • Raleigh, North Carolina

Pragmatic
Bookshelf

Many of the designations used by manufacturers and sellers to distinguish their products are claimed as trademarks. Where those designations appear in this book, and The Pragmatic Programmers, LLC was aware of a trademark claim, the designations have been printed in initial capital letters or in all capitals. The Pragmatic Starter Kit, The Pragmatic Programmer, Pragmatic Programming, Pragmatic Bookshelf, PragProg and the linking *g* device are trademarks of The Pragmatic Programmers, LLC.

Every precaution was taken in the preparation of this book. However, the publisher assumes no responsibility for errors or omissions, or for damages that may result from the use of information (including program listings) contained herein.

Our Pragmatic courses, workshops, and other products can help you and your team create better software and have more fun. For more information, as well as the latest Pragmatic titles, please visit us at *http://pragprog.com*.

The team that produced this book includes:

Brian P. Hogan (editor)
Candace Cunningham (copyeditor)
David J Kelly (typesetter)
Janet Furlow (producer)
Juliet Benda (rights)
Ellie Callahan (support)

Printed in the United States of America.
ISBN-13: 978-1-937785-74-1
Printed on acid-free paper.
Book version: P2.0—January 2014

Contents

Acknowledgments

In many ways, I consider writing a book very similar to writing code. Like writing code, writing a good book depends on the combined efforts of many people. I could not have completed this project without the help of my colleagues, family, and publisher.

Thank you to Joe Moore, Jay Hayes, and Justin Searls for sharing their experiences with remote pair programming. These folks were extremely generous with their time, and I highly recommend you pair with them if you have the chance.

I would also like to thank my reviewers: Ernie Miller, Avdi Grimm, Chad Taylor, Chris Johnson, Mark Anderson, Matt Blackmon, Nathan Claburn, Wilson Leong, and Vamsi Krishna Jandhyala. This is a first-class group of professionals who I'm proud to call my friends. Their insight and feedback helped shape this book's direction.

I must also thank my generous publisher. This is my third book with The Pragmatic Bookshelf, and I couldn't imagine having written it for anyone else. Thank you to Brian P. Hogan, Susannah Pfalzer, David Kelly, Andy Hunt, and Dave Thomas. As always, you have been remarkably supportive and helpful along the way.

Finally, thank you to my family. My wife and son are the reason I get up in the morning and stay up late at night to work on projects like this. Without their love and support, I'd probably get lost in my own house.

Preface

In March 2013, Yahoo! CEO Marissa Mayer sent a companywide memo that banned employees from working at home. She wrote, "To become the absolute best place to work, communication and collaboration will be important, so we need to work side-by-side."[1]

Mayer's motivations for making this now-infamous decision have been debated ad finem. It may or may not have been the right move for Yahoo!, but one thing is clear: working side-by-side does not require physical presence.

In this book, you'll learn how to collaborate with remote coworkers in ways that are better than sharing the same location. You'll learn about tools so powerful that colocated pair programming teams often use them despite sitting side-by-side. The technologies that make this possible can increase your productivity and the quality of the code you produce. But without them, you may face the problems that concerned Marissa Mayer.

In the months following Mayer's announcement, she defended her decision by saying, "People are more productive when they work alone...they're more collaborative and innovative when they're together."[2] Again, Mayer's premise may be correct, but innovation can happen from any location when you have the right people, processes, and technologies.

Those are three keystones of effective remote pair programming: people, process, and technology. Throughout this book, we'll discuss how you can master the techniques of remote pair programming by using the best tools, integrating those tools into your organizational process, and accommodating each person's individual needs. We'll also discuss scientific research that provides evidence of the benefits or pair programming, and warns of many common pitfalls.

---

1. http://money.cnn.com/2013/02/25/technology/yahoo-work-from-home/index.html
2. http://tech.fortune.cnn.com/2013/04/19/marissa-mayer-telecommuting/

Remote pair programming can open the door to a more diverse workforce, happier programmers, increased levels of innovation, and the freedom to work from any location. But this book isn't just for programmers outside the office.

Who Should Read This Book?

Every programmer, whether working remotely or from an office, can benefit from the technologies and advice discussed in this book. Being physically remote is an optional part of remote pair programming, and many colocated developers prefer the techniques discussed in this book to sharing a physical space.

Traditional pair programming requires sharing a computer, which means you're also sharing a keyboard, mouse, and everything else you touch. The close proximity also means you share germs, viruses, and odors. But pair programming with remote techniques, even if you sit within speaking distance of your pairing partner, can make the experience more comfortable and productive.

The technologies covered in this book favor a certain type of developer—one who is comfortable with the command line. The techniques and tools you'll learn about are not limited to the terminal, but command-line tools are favored because they tend to require less bandwidth and handle high-latency networks better than many other mediums.

As a result, some of the techniques we'll discuss simply won't work with frameworks like .NET or iOS. But it's still possible, and desirable, to employ remote pair programming on applications that use these frameworks. All of the tools you'll need are discussed in this book, and many of the tools that are not applicable can be tweaked to suit your needs. For example, we'll discuss how to create an Elastic Compute Cloud (EC2) instance running Linux, but the same principles apply if you need a server running Windows. The book even contains alternate paths in many chapters for readers that are running Windows. No matter what platform you favor or what technologies you're working with, this book will have something for you.

If you're a remote worker, or if the people you work with are dispersed across the country, then you'll gain the most from this book. We'll discuss how to solve problems of latency, bandwidth, security, and connectivity. But the same techniques apply regardless of your location.

Why Should You Read This Book?

Pair programming can be emotionally draining. You have to cooperate with other programmers, their personal preferences, and their schedules. But making these compromises can greatly increase the quality of the products you create, and it can hone your technical skills. You have to ensure that you don't burn out, and with the right techniques you won't.

The most common causes of pair-programming burnout are technical issues. If you spend an hour before a pairing session just trying to get connected or if your connection drops midsession, then you're going to grow weary. Likewise, if you're using a textual editor that gives one half of the pairing team too much control, you might grow tired of feeling that you are not contributing to the work product.

In this book, you'll learn about networking techniques, textual editors, and many other tools that make the practice of pairing fun. They will eliminate the technical challenges that drain your energy.

What's in This Book?

This book covers three major paradigms of remote pair programming: text-only collaboration, screen sharing, and integrated development environment (IDE) collaboration.

We'll begin with a general discussion on pair programming in Chapter 1, *Introduction to Pair Programming*, on page 1. You'll learn some rules of etiquette, scientific research, and how these apply to a remote environment.

We'll address the first major paradigm in Chapter 2, *Collaborating with Text Only*, on page 11. You'll learn to use command-line tools for sharing and collaboratively editing a code base with another programmer across the Internet. We'll follow up with Chapter 3, *Using the Cloud to Connect*, on page 27, where you'll learn some tools and techniques for making reliable and secure connections with your partner.

In Chapter 4, *Collaborating with Shared Screens*, on page 43, we'll discuss the next major paradigm. You'll learn how to share your entire screen, but you'll also learn how to share just the parts you're using. Each method is appropriate in certain situations, which you'll learn about. Many commercial tools make screen sharing easy, but we'll focus on the free and open source technologies.

In Chapter 5, *Building a Pairing Server*, on page 55, we'll put some tools together and build a complete pairing server that can be easily re-created, updated, shared, and destroyed. It can also create a more balanced experience for you and your partner.

We'll cover the last paradigm in Chapter 6, *Collaborating with an IDE*, on page 71. You'll learn about a robust pairing technology that runs within an IDE and how you can use it to reduce lag, increase responsiveness, and collaborate through many different interfaces.

Finally, we'll take a look at some real-world examples in Chapter 7, *Remote Pairing in the Wild*, on page 79. You'll learn how some of the most experienced programmers are using remote pairing to make their work better. We'll also discuss patterns you can use to provide structure in your pairing sessions.

What Do You Need to Use This Book?

An important tenet of pair programming is that it should accommodate a wide range of people and preferences. You should be able to pair-program with a partner who uses different tools than yours. That's why this book emphasizes cross-platform solutions. Many of the tools we'll discuss can be used from Mac, Linux, and even Windows. However, some of the tools favor certain platforms over others.

If you're running on Mac or Linux, you'll need to have a terminal-based editor installed. The examples we'll use favor Vim, but Emacs or any other solution will work. You'll also need a package manager, which is provided for you on most Linux systems, but you will need to install Homebrew on Mac OS X.[3]

If you're running Windows, you'll need a shell environment that supports SSH. Two great options are PuTTY,[4] a free implementation of SSH, and the Secure Shell plug-in for the Chrome browser.[5]

Regardless of your operating system, you'll need to install Vagrant, a virtual machine manager. Vagrant uses Oracle's VirtualBox to create virtual environments, so begin by downloading the VirtualBox installer from the Oracle site, and run it.[6] To install Vagrant, download and install the binary package for your platform from the Vagrant website, and run it.[7]

We can check that Vagrant was installed correctly by running the vagrant command like this:

---

3. http://brew.sh/
4. http://www.chiark.greenend.org.uk/~sgtatham/putty/
5. https://chrome.google.com/webstore/detail/secure-shell/pnhechapfaindjhompbnflcldabbghjo?hl=en
6. http://www.virtualbox.org/wiki/Downloads
7. http://downloads.vagrantup.com/

```
$ vagrant --version
Vagrant version 1.2.3
```

We'll use Vagrant throughout the book to create and configure pair-programming environments.

The next tool we'll need is RubyGems, which comes preinstalled with many Linux distributions (including the one we'll use with Vagrant) and even Mac OS X. You can check that it's available on your system by running this command:

```
$ gem -v
2.1.5
```

If the gem command does not work, you can install RubyGems with your system's package manager. On Debian-based Linux systems, run this command:

```
$ apt-get install ruby1.9.1
```

On Windows, download and follow the instructions for RubyInstaller.[8]

Those are the prerequisites, but there is one more thing you might want.

Having a Partner Is Optional

All of the examples in this book can be run without a partner, and we'll discuss tricks for testing these techniques without the assistance of another human. In most cases you won't even need a second computer, but in a few examples you may find it helpful to have an extra machine.

There will, however, come a time when you want to put the techniques in this book into action. Fortunately, a number of resources can help you find a partner. But the most convenient partner is probably a coworker.

When it comes to your coworkers, the best way to initiate a pairing session is to create an environment that is conducive to collaboration, and let partnership form organically. If the tools you need are right in front of you, then a session often evolves from a simple conversation about a piece of code. If your tools are not ready, the energy you need to pair will often fade before your environment is set up.

To be more deliberate when creating a session, you might head to your office's common area, log in to a chat room, or stick your head over a cubical wall and say, "Hey, anyone wanna pair?" It may work, but it's not the most formal

---

8. http://rubyinstaller.org/

way of starting a session. On the other hand, scheduling pairing sessions in advance may not work for some teams. Ultimately, the best way to get coworkers into a remote pair programming session will be different for every work environment. If your office is already using a system to schedule meetings and other events, then it might make sense to follow those same guidelines.

If you don't have a coworker or colleague to pair with, you can try using the #pairwithme tag on Twitter. Post a tweet describing what you'd like to work on, and a partner may reach out to you. Try something like "I want to dig into the Rails source code. Anyone want to #pairwithme?" Or you can look for programmers who have already posted a request to pair. There are some great aggregators for these requests.

The website at http://pair-with-me.herokuapp.com/ simply collects tweets that use the #pairwithme hash tag so you can browse or search them. There are also some technology-specific websites. The Ruby Pair website is helpful for linking up on projects using the Ruby programming language, while the Ember Pairs website is helpful for pairing on the Ember.js project.[9,10] The Pair Program with Me website provides dozens of other resources for finding a partner.[11]

Let's pair up.

---

9. http://rubypair.com/
10. http://www.emberpairs.com/
11. http://www.pairprogramwith.me/

CHAPTER 1

Introduction to Pair Programming

There is an old saying that two heads are better than one. It may not be universally true, but modern psychology research has provided evidence of its validity in many situations.[1] For programmers, an extra set of eyes can prevent errors and inject new ideas when working to solve tough problems. Writing code in conjunction with another programmer might help us identify edge cases or create better code designs that reduce coupling and improve cohesion—making our programs easier to maintain down the road. But there's no need to speculate about the benefits of writing code with another programmer. Evidence from academia and industry shows that pair programming leads to better code.[2]

Pair programming is a technique in which two programmers jointly produce one artifact, such as a design, an algorithm, or some code. Experiments have demonstrated that pairing improves design quality, reduces defects, reduces staffing risk, enhances technical skills, improves team communications, and is considered more enjoyable at statistically significant levels.[3]

Traditionally, a pairing team would sit physically side-by-side, but improvements to screen-sharing tools, terminal-based editors, and virtualization have made it easy for pairing teams to work from different locations. Even better, studies have concluded that the quality and time benefits of remote pairing are the same as when pairing traditionally. But not all pair programming is equal—you've got to follow the rules.

---

1. *Optimally Interacting Minds [BOLR10]*
2. *Strengthening the case for pair programming [WKCJ00]*
3. *The costs and benefits of pair programming [CW00]*

Laying the Ground Rules

No matter where you're pairing from or what tools you're using, you must follow these rules if you want to benefit from the technique.

Share Everything   If you are using a tool to debug some code, inspect a runtime, or anything else, your partner must be able to see it. In traditional pairing this usually means sharing the same physical computer. But in remote pairing it's more nuanced, and it's the primary problem we'll address in this book.

Share Equally   Your tools should not give one party a control advantage over the other. The best example of violating this in remote pairing is the use of view-only screen sharing.

Be Comfortable   In traditional pairing, comfort is usually a function of your physical surroundings. But in remote pairing it often depends on the quality of audio and video, or the general ability to communicate. For example, if you find it difficult to express that you need a bathroom break, you won't be comfortable.

Stop When You're Tired   Many programmers hate pair programming, and understandably so. It's exhausting. But you'll learn about tools that help reduce fatigue and make it easy to pair for longer periods of time. Even with these tools, however, it's important to stop when you become disengaged.

Debate with Your Partner (But Keep It Short)   Your pairing environment should be democratic, and you should be comfortable expressing your opinions. But you may be wasting time if the debate goes on for too long. Jeff Langr and Tim Ottinger, the authors of *Agile in a Flash: Speed-Learning Agile Software Development [LO11]*, recommend debating for no more than ten minutes without producing some code.

These are the rules, and they work. We know this because we have scientific evidence to prove it.

Examining the Evidence

In the mid 1990s, a number of software-engineering experts began to observe the growing trend of pairing in development teams. They reported that programmers were producing code faster and freer of bugs than ever before.[4]

---

4.   *Pattern Languages of Program Design 2 [VCK96]*

Around the same time, a group of Smalltalk programmers and software-engineering consultants began to incorporate this practice into a methodology they called extreme programming (XP).

As XP gained traction in the industry, software-engineering researchers began publishing the results of controlled experiments that compared the work products of paired and individual programmers. A 1998 study from Temple University found paired teams completed their tasks 40% faster than individuals doing the same work, and they produced better algorithms and code.[5] Subsequent studies confirmed these results.[6] Most of the experiments were conducted in a controlled academic environment, but the software industry at large was finding similar results.

In one example of real-world success, Ron Jeffries and Kent Beck introduced pair programming to a project for the Chrysler Corporation. Five months later, they found nearly all of the bugs making their way into the production system were written by solo programmers. The project was completed close to schedule and was ultimately deemed a great success.[7]

However, all of these early studies were focused on colocated pair programmers. We cannot just assume that the results will hold true for distributed teams. Fortunately, a number of other studies, which compare distributed pair programming (another name for remote pair programming) to traditional pairing, suggest that the same benefits exist. A 2002 study from North Carolina State University found distributed pair programming teams produced code of the same quality in the same amount of time as colocated teams.[8] More recent studies have confirmed these results.[9]

Not all pair-programming teams are equal, though. Some studies suggest that the expertise of the programmers and the complexity of the tasks may determine the technique's effectiveness. In some cases, it was found that junior programmers require more time when pairing on complex tasks, but still produce higher-quality code. Intermediate-level programmers seem to benefit the most from pairing. One study found that developers in this category experienced a massive 149% increase in correctness over individual programmers.[10] Expert programmers show varying levels of success depending

---

5. *The case for collaborative programming [Nos98]*
6. *Strengthening the case for pair programming [WKCJ00]*
7. *Chrysler Goes to 'Extremes' [ABB98]*
8. *Exploring the efficacy of distributed pair programming [BGS02]*
9. *Empirical evaluation of distributed pair programming [Han02]*
10. *The Effectiveness of Pair Programming: A Meta-Analysis [HDAS09]*

on the complexity of a task. But the worst case is breaking even. There is no evidence to suggest that quality or productivity will be reduced for any level of expertise or task complexity.

One potential drawback of pairing is that it may require additional effort to complete a task. Pairing teams produce faster results because they work in tandem, but the combined effort may lead to as much as a 60% increase in man-hours. Researchers have found, however, that this overhead may begin to subside after awhile. Programmers often go through a phase called "jelling" when they are first introduced to pairing. During this phase, teams may require 60% more man-hours to complete a task, but after the adjustment period it is often reduced to a minimum of 15%.[11] The same research, however, suggests teams can make up for this overhead in the long term because the quality of the code they produce, as measured by bugs, will be better.

It's believed that once a team jells, it becomes "almost unstoppable, a juggernaut for success," according to IEEE fellow Tom DeMarco.[12] Jelled teams also tend to enjoy tasks that individuals would consider dull. Thus, your goal when pairing is not simply to be in the company of another programmer, but to act as one with that person. It will always take time to jell, but when it comes to *remote* pairing there are additional concerns. To jell with a remote partner, you must take action at the beginning of each session to ensure the process goes smoothly.

Pairing Up

Regardless of who you're partnering with or what you'll be working on, each pairing session should begin with the following three steps.

Step One: Establish a Communication Channel

The communication channel can be as simple as an instant-messaging program, but it's usually preferable to have an audio and even a visual connection. You can use any of the many voice- and video-communication tools available, but we won't explore those in detail. If you don't know where to start, use Skype.[13] Its reputation as a user-friendly tool is weak, but its ubiquity and even the reliability of the voice over IP technology underlying the clunky client interface is unparalleled. We'll discuss Skype and some alternatives in more detail later in the chapter.

---

11. *Strengthening the case for pair programming [WKCJ00]*
12. *Peopleware: Productive Projects and Teams [DL99]*
13. http://www.skype.com/

Regardless of the voice software you choose, it's also important to have a good microphone. The mic included in your laptop or display will probably reduce the likelihood of your partner understanding your every word—and your partner *should* be able understand every word. If you're going to pair-program often, then get a moderately good microphone such as the Blue Snowball.[14] If you prefer a headset, consider the Logitech H390, which is affordable and has a good reputation.[15]

After getting connected, do a quick mic check. Make sure there is no background noise, static, lag, echo, or anything else that might make the other person difficult to hear. If you find a problem, address it immediately. Once you've established a good communication channel, you'll need to discuss a few things with your partner.

Step Two: Get Comfortable

If this is the first time you and your partner are pairing, you'll need to define your expectations well. You should discuss your experiences with remote pair programming and be clear about things that might make the process difficult for you. If you need to take frequent bathroom breaks, make it known. If you have low bandwidth or your connection is laggy, then tell your partner. Both you and your partner must be comfortable.

With the basic housekeeping out of the way, the next thing you'll need to establish is your goals. Be specific about what code you want to work on, and what you expect to accomplish. Many programmers like to identify specific tests that need to be fixed. Other times, the goal is to write tests to replicate bugs or define new features.

Step Three: Agree on Your Tools

Before you change a single line of code, you and your partner need to agree on the tools you'll use to do it. This includes operating system, text editors, integrated development environments, testing tools, debugging tools, and more. Choosing the right tools might be the most important part of pair programming, and that's why the majority of this book is dedicated to understanding the pros and cons of each option.

Regardless of your choice of development tools, you should be using a version-control system (VCS) for your code. Most VCSs record each commit, along with the author who made it. That is *author*, not *authors*. The first order of

---

14. http://bluemic.com/snowball/
15. http://www.logitech.com/en-us/product/stereo-headset-h390

business is telling your VCS that you're pair programming. Some excellent tools make this easier, but most of them work only with Git. Two such Git-based tools are Hitch and Sprout.

Hitch is a Ruby Gem for easily setting and resetting your configuration.[16] You can run commands like hitch jane john to get started and hitch -u to return your configuration to its defaults. The Sprout project from Pivotal Labs is a set of Chef cookbooks that include a pairing recipe.[17]

Tools like Hitch and Sprout are making it convenient to run these commands:

```
$ git config --global user.name "Jane Doe and John Smith"
$ git config --global user.email janedoe+johnsmith@example.com
```

You can always resort to running them yourself. You'll need to do something similar for Mercurial, svn, or whatever VCS you're using. But even after your VCS is set up, you still aren't ready to code. You need some remote-pairing development tools. Fortunately, that's what the rest of this book is about.

Getting Started with Some Basic Tools

Mary is an eight-year-old with spinal muscular atrophy. This rare condition confines her to a wheelchair and prevents her from attending school during flu season because of her weak immune system. But that doesn't stop Mary from participating in class and earning good grades. Mary's teacher has an iPad, which runs Apple's FaceTime and acts as a kind of virtual student in the classroom. At home, Mary connects to FaceTime with her iMac and uses other sharing technologies to view the teacher's electronic whiteboard in real time. It's a bit like remote pair programming without the code. Mary can get a lot done with just a few common tools, and the same is true for software developers.

Try each of the communication technologies in the following section and become familiar with their features. None of them fully satisfies the needs of remote pair programming, but they provide an essential foundation for building an environment in which you can collaborate with your partner.

Skype[18]

Skype was first introduced in 2003, and Microsoft purchased it in 2011. Some reviewers have called the client application "clunky and unpleasant to use,"[19]

---

16. https://github.com/therubymug/hitch
17. https://github.com/pivotal-sprout/sprout
18. http://www.skype.com/
19. http://www.macworld.com/article/2036311/review-skype-remains-a-fine-voip-video-chatting-option-on-ios.html

but that hasn't slowed its adoption. Skype handles more international phone calls than AT&T.[20]

If you don't have a Skype client on your machine, go download it now. You will eventually need it even if you don't use it day-to-day. Then find a friend and try voice calling, video calling, and screen sharing. Share your development tools with a partner. You may be able to accomplish some basic tasks, but you'll probably feel limited. Skype's screen sharing does not provide two-way control, and it consumes a lot of bandwidth.

If you simply can't stand Skype after trying it, move on to one of these similar communication options: Google Voice,[21] Apple FaceTime,[22] or Ekiga.[23] All of these tools handle audio and video, while Google Voice and Apple FaceTime support basic screen sharing as well. But another class of communication tools goes even further.

Google Hangouts[24]

Google Hangouts was released in May 2013 and has made huge inroads during its short lifetime.[25] Hangouts is a communication platform that supports instant messaging, video chat, screen sharing, and more. It's quickly become popular with programmers as a means of sharing screens and pair programming.

Two Ruby developers, Avdi Grimm and Josh Susser, recorded a screencast of a pairing session they conducted over Hangouts.[26] Their video provides an excellent example of the main advantages and disadvantages of Hangouts. Avdi and Josh were easily able to share Avdi's integrated development environment, but only Avdi could directly control the environment. Josh's role was constrained to that of a navigator or researcher. Some teams find this acceptable, but in *Patterns of Pairing*, on page 85, we'll discuss why we must exercise caution when assigning roles in this way.

Google recently added a Remote Desktop feature to Hangouts allowing for two-way control of a session, but it has severe limitations with regard to screen size. Each session is limited to the size of the main Hangout window,

---

20. http://arstechnica.com/tech-policy/2009/03/skype-handles-more-international-calls-than-att/

21. https://www.google.com/voice#inbox

22. http://www.apple.com/mac/facetime/

23. http://ekiga.org/

24. https://plus.google.com/hangouts

25. http://arstechnica.com/information-technology/2013/05/google-beefs-up-hangouts-into-text-photo-video-chat-powerhouse/

26. http://www.youtube.com/watch?v=8LUIqm6xy8A

which makes it difficult to see details and read code. It may be useful for quick or simple tasks, such as helping your family remove Spyware, but it's not adequate for pair-programming.

A few developers have created tools that quickly spin up Hangout sessions and create a URL that you can share with your partner. One in particular uses Alfred,[27] a Mac OS X utility, to put a Hangout URL directly into your system clipboard, which you can then easily paste into a chat session.[28]

Screenhero[29]

The final technology we'll discuss, Screenhero, is a commercial collaborative screen-sharing application that lets you share individual windows. It's so new that it's still beta software, but it's becoming a major player in the market for remote development tools. Because the sharing can be limited to a single window, the shared application feels almost native. Another advantage of Screenhero is that each user gets his own mouse. Your partner can point to a location on the screen without stealing control from you, and visa versa. Download Screenhero right now—it's free while it's in beta.

Screenhero does a good job of handling the technical challenges of remote pair programming, but it's not without disadvantages. It doesn't support Linux, and it still requires lots of bandwidth. You will likely experience occasional lag and pixelation.

Many remote pair programmers use nothing more than tools like Screenhero, Google Hangouts, and Skype to support their work. But if you want to get the most out of your pair-programming sessions and realize the benefits described in *Examining the Evidence*, on page 2, you'll need something more. All of these tools have the same problems: they consume lots of bandwidth, they are often laggy, and they depend heavily on the availability of a third party (that is, if that party's servers go down, then you can't work). Furthermore, Skype and Google Hangouts lack adequate two-way control, which violates one of the rules we discussed at the beginning of the chapter.

The biggest difference between Mary's remote environment and our desired remote pair programming environment is that we must function as peers. Both programmers must be able to control the environment equally and contribute to the code base. The tools you've learned about in this chapter simply don't live up to this demand (although Screenhero comes very close).

---

27. http://www.alfredapp.com/

28. http://blog.jonathanrwallace.com/blog/2013/10/08/quickly-create-a-google-hangout-with-alfred/

29. http://screenhero.com/

That doesn't mean you should avoid remote pairing with these tools, but it's best to use them as a supplement to more powerful tools that suit the needs of a software developer. In the coming chapters, you'll learn about tools that solve all the problems we've discussed.

What's Next?

You've learned why some of the best software companies in the world tout pair programming. The evidence of its benefits is undeniable, but creating an environment in which a pairing team can jell requires discipline and some good tools. You've set up a basic pair-programming environment with Skype, Google Hangouts, or Screenhero. But these tools are not enough—and they will fall down in some situations.

We'll spend the next several chapters discussing more programming tools, configuration options, and networking techniques that aid in remote pair programming. Let's get to work.

CHAPTER 2

Collaborating with Text Only

Let's imagine we've found a bug in the open source library Backbone.js, a code base that we aren't very familiar with. We post a tweet such as "Found a memory leak in Backbone.js. Anyone want to #pairwithme and fix it?" Because we used the #pairwithme hash tag, someone with the same problem replies and wants to pair-program with us to fix it. Now what?

We need a way to share the Backbone.js source code and collaboratively modify it with our partner. Many commercial screen-sharing applications and advanced integrated development environments (IDEs) make this possible. But not every programmer will have access to those specialized tools or even enough bandwidth to use them. Because we must quickly connect with a new partner, our collaborative editing environment must be ubiquitous, unobtrusive, and lightweight. We need a terminal-based stack of tools that can share a minimal text-based view of our code. Even if you prefer screen sharing or an IDE, the terminal will always be the most reliable platform for pairing, and knowing how to use it is essential.

Terminal-based tools typically require less bandwidth and handle high-latency networks better than screen-sharing applications. Their primitive nature also makes them more accessible than IDEs because they use readily available platforms and protocols. That doesn't make them any less useful, though. Programmers at companies such as Pivotal Labs, Thoughtbot, Braintree, and Relevance use terminal-based editors as their tools of choice for remote pairing.[1,2,3,4] The technology underpinning many of their terminal-based environments is tmux.

---

1. http://pivotallabs.com/how-we-use-tmux-for-remote-pair-programming/
2. http://robots.thoughtbot.com/post/2641409235/a-tmux-crash-course
3. https://www.braintreepayments.com/braintrust/vimux-simple-vim-and-tmux-integration
4. http://thinkrelevance.com/blog/tags/tmux

tmux is a terminal multiplexer that's used to manage multiple windows, and share editors like Emacs and Vim. We can run a database console, web server, and text editor side-by-side in separate panes. We can also can connect multiple tmux clients to the same session so a pairing partner can see and interact with these windows.

You'll learn the basics of tmux as we hack on the Backbone.js source code. Backbone is a client-side model-view-controller framework built in JavaScript, and it presents some interesting pairing problems because it runs in a browser, which can't be shared via tmux. In the process of fixing that problem, you'll learn how to use tmux with your own projects.

Before we dig into the code, let's set up our development environment for pairing.

Installing tmux

On Linux, we can download tmux from the system's package manager. The command on Debian-based systems like Ubuntu is this:

```
$ apt-get install tmux
```

On CentOS- and RedHat-based Linux systems the command is this:

```
$ yum install tmux
```

On Mac OS X, we can install it with the help of Homebrew by using the following command:

```
$ brew install tmux
```

However, the versions of tmux that apt-get and yum provide will be out of date. If we want to use the latest and greatest tmux, then we'll need to follow the steps to compile it in *Installing tmux from Source*, on page 13. But as long as we're running version 1.7 or newer, the examples in this book will work.

Running tmux on Windows

We can't run tmux natively on Windows, but we can run it in a virtual machine. Vagrant, which we installed in the *Preface*, on page ix, makes it possible to run tmux on Windows in just a few steps. Create a tmux directory, and move into it. Then add a new virtual machine by running these commands:

```
C:\tmux> vagrant box add precise32 http://files.vagrantup.com/precise32.box
C:\tmux> vagrant init precise32
C:\tmux> vagrant up
```

Now you can run the following command to log into the virtual machine if you have SSH on your path (you will if you have Git installed).

`C:\tmux>` **`vagrant ssh`**

If the ssh command does not work, open either PuTTY or the Secure Shell extension for Chrome, which we also installed in the *Preface*, on page ix. Then create a new SSH connection to your host, 127.0.0.1, on port 2222. The login credentials are *vagrant* for the username and *vagrant* for the password.

Whether you connected with the vagrant ssh command or a third-party tool, you'll see this prompt:

`vagrant@precise32:~$`

From here, we can run all of the commands described in this chapter. But as with any native Linux installation, the package manager may not give us the latest version of tmux. If we want that, we'll need to compile it from source.

Installing tmux from Source

To install tmux from source, we'll need a GCC compiler. On Mac OS X, install the command-line tools in Xcode by going to Preferences, selecting the Downloads tab, and pressing Install next to the Command Line Tools item.

On Linux, we'll use the package manager again. The command for Ubuntu is as follows:

`$ ` **`sudo apt-get install build-essential`**

We'll also need a few libraries tmux depends upon. Install them on Ubuntu with this command:

`$ ` **`sudo apt-get install libevent-dev libncurses-dev`**

Now that we have these prerequisites installed, download the tmux source from the official website with this command on a Mac:[5]

`$ ` **`curl -OL http://downloads.sourceforge.net/tmux/tmux-1.8.tar.gz`**

Or this command on Linux (including a Vagrant box):

`$ ` **`wget http://downloads.sourceforge.net/tmux/tmux-1.8.tar.gz`**

Then untar the archive, compile the code it contains, and install tmux like this:

5.　http://tmux.sourceforge.net/

```
$ tar -zxvf tmux-1.8.tar.gz
$ cd tmux-1.8
$ ./configure
$ make
$ sudo make install
```

Whether you installed tmux from source or from a package manager, check that it's working by running the tmux command like so:

```
$ tmux -V
tmux 1.8
```

Now let's kick the tires a bit. We'll explore the basics of tmux in solo mode before pairing up with a partner.

Using tmux as a Solo Programmer

Start a tmux session with the tmux command, like so:

```
$ tmux
```

You'll notice a slight change to your terminal, such that it looks like the following figure.

Figure 1—An empty tmux session

This is a tmux session. We can do anything from this terminal that we might do in a regular terminal session, such as edit files with Emacs or Vim. If you're familiar with these editors, try one out right now.

The tmux session consists of a window that contains the terminal, and a status bar that displays the window's name and some other information. We can divide the window into multiple panes that allow us to view more than one thing at a time. Let's split the window vertically.

In the tmux session, press Ctrl-b, release, and then press %. The window will be divided down the middle, creating two panes. The left pane is our original terminal session, and the right pane contains a new terminal session. If we were running a program like Vim or Emacs, then it would still be running in the left pane. We can switch focus between the left and right sides by pressing Ctrl-b and then o.

Now switch focus back to the left pane, close any programs may have been running, and enter the following command to start the top application.

```
$ top
```

We'll see something like the following figure.

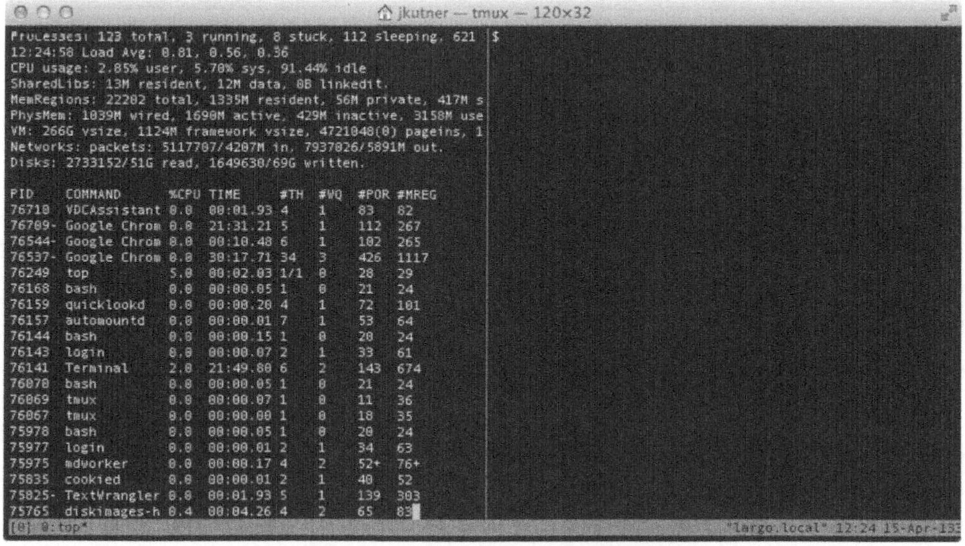

Figure 2—Running **top** in a tmux pane

top monitors the memory and CPU usage of the processes running on our computer. We'll even see tmux in the list. Now switch focus to the right pane, and start a new process by entering the following command:

```
$ ping google.com
```

We'll see output that looks like the following figure, with ping running in the right pane as it sends packets to google.com. We'll also see its activity in top.

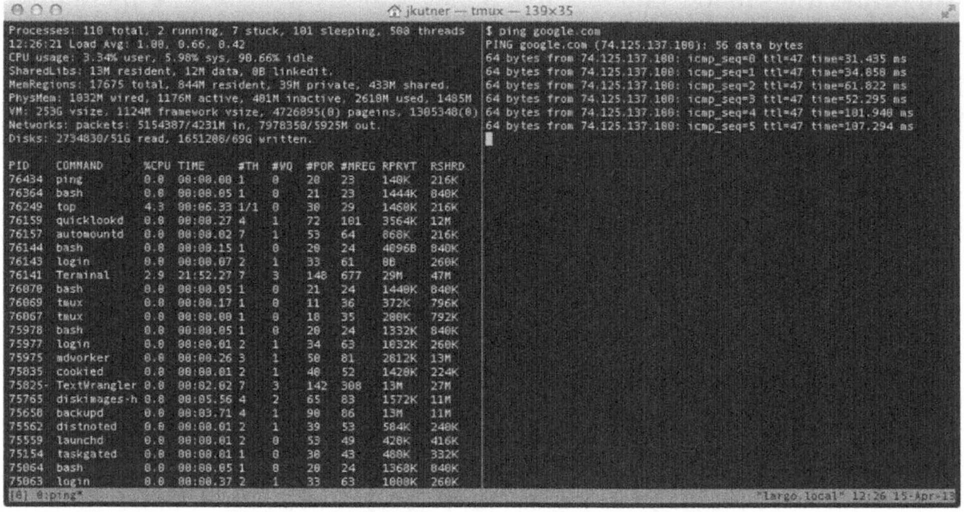

Figure 3—Monitoring ping with top and tmux

In addition to creating new panes, we can create new windows by pressing Ctrl-b c. Do this now, and you'll see a new terminal session. The top and ping processes are still running, but they're in the background. We can switch back to them by pressing Ctrl-b 0 or Ctrl-b 1, where 0 and 1 correspond to the number associated with the window in the menu bar at the bottom of the session.

This is just a simple example of how useful tmux can be to our development process. We can create more panes that run web servers, database clients, and text editors. I highly recommend that you educate yourself on tmux's many features, and *tmux: Productive Mouse-Free Development [Hog12]* is an excellent resource. But expertise is not necessary to start using tmux for pairing. For the purpose of this book, we'll focus on the parts of tmux that are essential to remote pair programming.

Before we move on, let's close one of the panes. Press Ctrl-b x from the pane that's running ping. We will be prompted to answer (y/n) before it actually closes. Press y. This will kill the ping process, and we'll see only the top program again. Exit it by pressing Ctrl-c.

Next, we'll create a tmux session that we can share with our pairing partner.

Sharing a tmux Session

To pair-program with tmux, we must connect a second client to our session. Leave the tmux session we created earlier running. Then open a second terminal window (outside of tmux) and run this command:

```
$ tmux attach
```

The second terminal will look identical to the first terminal. That's because it's the same tmux session. Start typing in the first terminal, and we'll see the changes in the second terminal. Likewise, characters entered in the second terminal will appear in the first terminal. If we run a command like ping, it will be visible in both consoles. We're only simulating the process of pair programming with tmux in this example. In the real world, the two terminal windows would exist on separate machines, but the result would be the same: a collaborative editing environment.

You may have noticed when connecting a second client to the tmux session that the window is only as big as the smallest terminal, as the following figure shows.

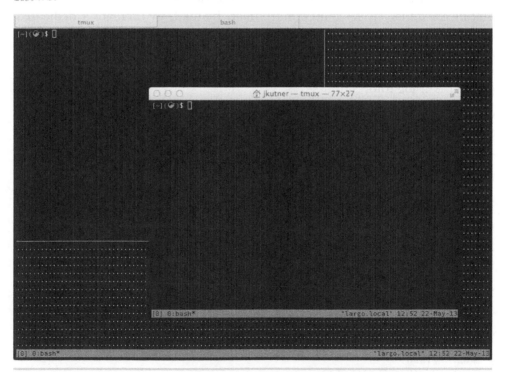

Figure 4—Two tmux windows with different sizes

This is good because it means that both programmers are seeing the exact same thing. But sometimes resizing a terminal that contains a tmux window can cause all sorts of weird display issues. If this happens, just detach the misbehaving client by pressing Ctrl-b d, and reattach with the same command we ran earlier. tmux version 1.8 has reflow support, which largely eliminates this problem.

Now, detach the second session by pressing Ctrl-b and then d in tmux. The second terminal will return to the normal prompt, but the first terminal will remain in the tmux session. Anyone using the same user account as us can rejoin this session with the attach command.

But don't forget that we're going to pair with a programmer we found on Twitter. We don't want that person logging in with our user account. Let's discuss how to securely share this session.

Sharing Sessions Across User Accounts

We could share a tmux session by creating a joint user account that both parties log into, but we would lose all of our dotfiles and any tools we have installed exclusively for our primary user. Instead, we'll create a dedicated account for our pairing partner, and share a tmux session between that account and our primary user account. Some people create a user specifically for each pairing partner, but we'll just create a general tmux user that any partner can log into.

On Mac OS X, create a *tmux* user from the Users & Groups section in the System Preferences application, as Figure 5, *Creating a tmux user on Mac OS X*, on page 19 shows.

On Ubuntu and many other Linux systems, create the tmux user like this:

```
$ adduser tmux
```

Next, we'll give our pairing partner access to this account. Emailing a password is not very safe, so we'll use an SSH key. Switch to the tmux user by running this command:

```
$ su tmux
```

Then create a .ssh and the .ssh/authorized_keys file, setting the appropriate permissions. Only the tmux user should be allowed to read, write, or execute this.

```
$ mkdir ~/.ssh
$ touch ~/.ssh/authorized_keys
$ chmod 700 ~/.ssh
$ chmod 600 ~/.ssh/authorized_keys
```

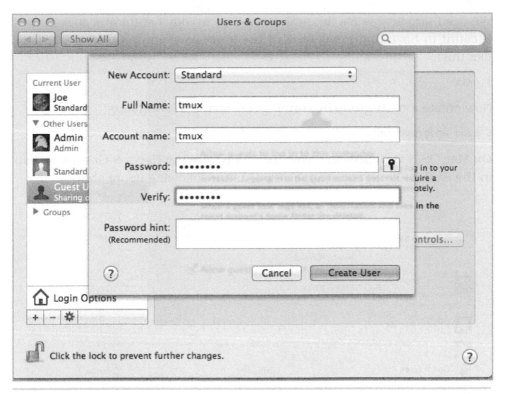

Figure 5—Creating a tmux user on Mac OS X

Next, we'll add our partner's public key to the authorized_keys file. If our partner has a GitHub account, we can use the github-auth Ruby Gem to help us.[6] We installed RubyGems in the *Preface*, on page ix, so we can download and install github-auth with this command:

```
$ gem install github-auth
```

This will add the gh-auth script to our path. We can test it out by adding our own public key like this (replace johndoe with your GitHub username):

```
$ gh-auth add --users=johndoe
Adding 2 key(s) to '/Users/tmux/.ssh/authorized_keys'
```

We could repeat the command with our partner's GitHub username, but we'll skip that step since our partner is imaginary. When we're done with the partner, we can remove her key with the gh-auth remove command.

---

6.   https://github.com/chrishunt/github-auth

We need sudo access for the next steps, but we don't want our guest's user account to have that privilege. Exit the tmux user and return to your user like this:

```
$ exit
```

Now create a *tmux* group by running this command on Linux:

```
$ sudo addgroup tmux
```

On Mac OS X we'll need to create the group from the Users & Groups section in the System Preferences application, as the following figure shows.

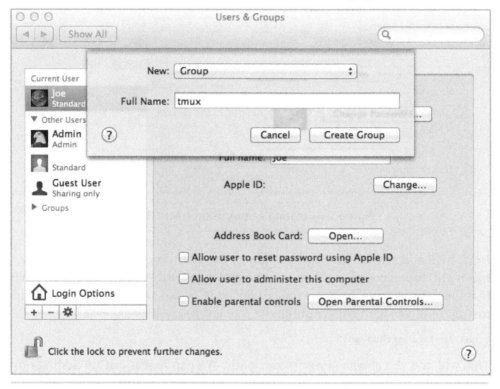

Figure 6—Creating a tmux group on Mac OS X

Now create a /var/tmux directory to hold our shared sessions and change its ownership so the tmux group has access.

```
$ sudo mkdir /var/tmux
$ sudo chgrp tmux /var/tmux
```

Then alter the folder permissions so that new files will be accessible for all members of the tmux group:

```
$ sudo chmod g+ws /var/tmux
```

Finally, add both the tmux user and our user to the tmux group. On Linux, run these commands (replace janedoe with your username):

```
$ sudo usermod -aG tmux tmux
$ sudo usermod -aG tmux janedoe
```

On some systems, including the Vagrant box, we'll have to log out and log back in for these user changes to take effect.

On Mac OS X, we can add the users to the tmux group in Users & Groups, as the following figure shows.

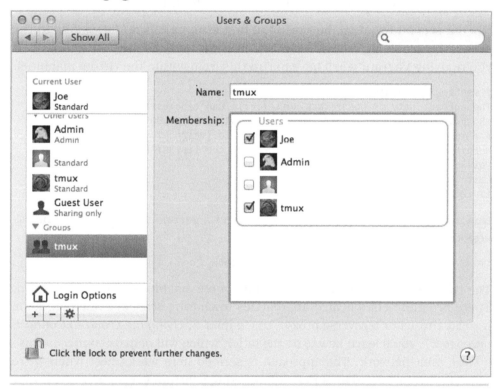

Figure 7—Adding users to the tmux group on Mac OS X

Finally, we must give the tmux user remote login access. On Linux, this is enabled by default. On Mac OS X, open the Sharing section from the System Preferences application and select the Remote Login option from the list of services. Check the box next to it, and select the "All Users" option from the panel on the right-side. If you prefer to give access only to specific users, then you must add the tmux user to the list at the bottom of the panel.

In the next section, we'll create a tmux session that we can share between these two users.

Sharing tmux Sessions with Sockets

If a tmux session is running, terminate it by entering exit in the console. Then run the following command, which will create a pair socket (essentially just a file) under the /var/tmux directory:

```
$ tmux -S /var/tmux/pair
```

The new tmux session will look identical to our old ones, but now a tmux client from another user account can connect to it. Let's do just that.

Open a second terminal, but keep the first terminal open and visible. In the second terminal, log in with the tmux user just as a remote partner would (if you're using Vagrant you'll have to run this from within the virtual machine).

```
$ ssh tmux@localhost
The authenticity of host 'localhost (::1)' can't be established.
RSA key fingerprint is 00:00:00:00:00:00:00:00:00:00:00:00:00:00:00:00.
Are you sure you want to continue connecting (yes/no)? yes
Warning: Permanently added 'host' (RSA) to the list of known hosts.
Password:
Last login: Fri Mar 29 09:52:08 2013
tmux@localhost$
```

Now run this command, which will connect a second tmux client to the pair session.

```
tmux@localhost$ tmux -S /var/tmux/pair attach
```

The two sessions, which are simulating remote machines, will be connected. There are more-complicated approaches to sharing sessions, such as using a socat tunnel or a reverse proxy.[7] In Chapter 3, *Using the Cloud to Connect*, on page 27, you'll learn how to do the latter, which will help us connect across a wide area network. The approach described here works best when we're sharing across a local area network or using a virtual private network.

Now let's move on to the code.

Using tmux for Pairing

With both of our tmux windows in a good working state as we left them in the previous section, let's check out the Backbone.js code base. Run this command from either tmux terminal:

---

7. http://thread.gmane.org/gmane.comp.terminal-emulators.tmux.user/579

```
$ git clone git@github.com:documentcloud/backbone.git
```

Move into the newly created backbone directory and open the file test/model.js in any terminal-based editor, as you can see here:

```
$ cd backbone
$ vim test/model.js
```

This file contains some unit tests for Backbone's model components. We can run these test by opening the test/index.html file in a browser. Split the tmux session horizontally by pressing Ctrl-b ", so that your window looks like the following figure.

Figure 8—The Backbone.js code in tmux

Then run this command in the new pane (you'll have to skip this step if you're using Vagrant, because it doesn't have a browser):

```
$ open test/index.html
```

A browser will open and the JavaScript tests will run, as the following figure shows. There's just one problem: our partner can't see the browser because it's not a part of the tmux session.

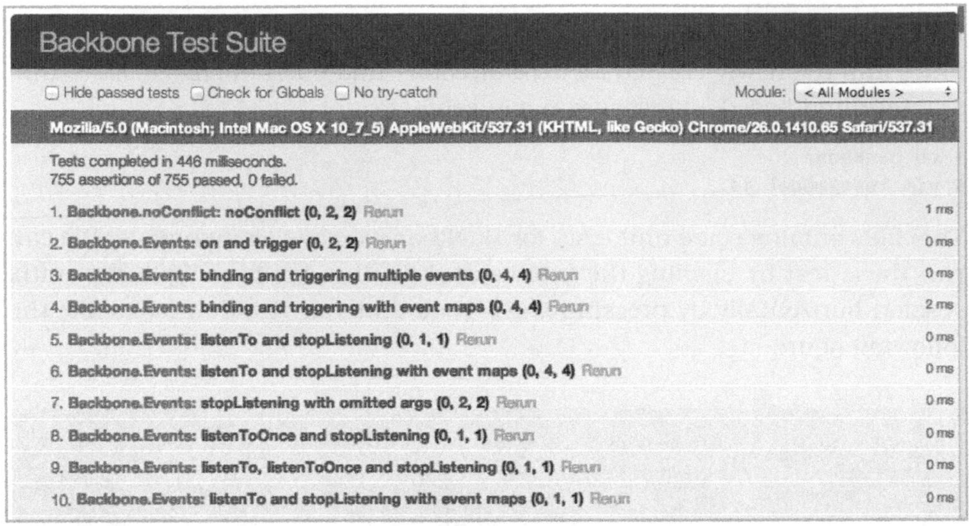

Figure 9—Testing Backbone.js in a browser

There are many ways to share a browser, and some other ways of solving the problem without sharing a browser. The simplest solution is view-only screen sharing. If we are already using Skype or one of the similar tools we discussed in Chapter 1, *Introduction to Pair Programming*, on page 1, then we can do this with the click of a button. View-only screen sharing is acceptable in this scenario because we aren't actually controlling the browser. We're only letting it run our tests. But screen sharing uses a lot of bandwidth just to watch some tests run. Wouldn't it be better if we could run the tests in the tmux session? We can with a headless browser engine like PhantomJS.

PhantomJS is an implementation of WebKit that can be run from the terminal for jobs like running unit tests. On Mac OS X we can install it with brew by running this command:

```
$ brew install phantomjs
```

For Linux and Windows, download the binary for your platform from the official PhantomJS website and follow the installation instructions.[8] Regardless of the platform, we can run this command to test that the installation was successful:

```
$ phantomjs -v
1.9.0
```

---

8. http://phantomjs.org/

Now return to our tmux session. In the bottom pane, run the command shown here:

```
$ phantomjs test/vendor/runner.js test/index.html
Took 363ms to run 755 tests. 755 passed, 0 failed.
```

The test/vendor/runner.js is a script for kicking off the unit tests in the index.html. Now both tmux users can watch them run.

Using terminal-based tools like tmux and PhantomJS is important when pair-programming because they require less bandwidth, have lower latency, and are usually easier to connect. But they won't solve all of our problems. We have to be creative when pairing from the terminal, and sometimes we just need a graphical interface. In the coming chapters, we'll explore some ways of doing this by sharing control of our screen.

What's Next?

You've learned about some essential pair-programming tools. The ability to collaborate entirely from the terminal is important, and a kind of lowest common denominator for pairing. But the application of these tools is not limited to pair programming. Many developers use tmux, PhantomJS, and, of course, Vim in their daily solo programming.

You may find that it helps to try additional tools that either supplement or replace tmux and Vim. I've listed a few suggestions here:

GNU Screen[9] An aging full-screen window manager that multiplexes terminals among processes in a way similar to tmux. It includes a few unique features, such as file transfers with the zmodem protocol, but it lacks some tmux features, such as vertical window-splitting.

CoVim[10] A plug-in that adds real-time collaboration features to the Vim text editor. Its maintainers describe it as "Google Docs for Vim." CoVim enables features that are similar to tmux's, but it lacks support for tools outside of Vim—such as a shared command prompt.

wemux[11] A Mac OS X tool that enhances tmux to make multiuser terminal multiplexing both easier and more powerful. It allows users to host a wemux server and have clients join in various modes that support mirroring, shared cursors, and separate cursors.

---

9.   http://www.gnu.org/software/screen/
10. https://github.com/FredKSchott/CoVim
11. https://github.com/zolrath/wemux

ls-pair[12] The programmers at LivingSocial, a daily-deal website, created this small set of tools as a baseline environment for doing remote pair programming via SSH. It consists of wemux, a default configuration for tmux and Vim, and a few other niceties.

All of these terminal-based tools, including tmux and Vim, have their limitations, though. They won't help us share graphics or visual components of our applications. They are optimized to work best without a mouse, and they require that both programmers share relatively strong skills with the same terminal-based editor. If you know how to use only Vim and your partner knows how to use only Emacs, then you'll likely be hamstrung by the difficulty of one party learning a new system. In Chapter 6, *Collaborating with an IDE*, on page 71, we'll discuss how to use editors that don't suffer from this problem.

But first, let's go to a café and continue our tmux session over a cup of coffee. In the next chapter, you'll learn how to pair-program from any location on the planet, including cafés with heavily locked-down routers.

---

12. https://github.com/livingsocial/ls-pair

CHAPTER 3

Using the Cloud to Connect

Let's imagine we're taking our laptop to a café to get a high-quality espresso. Most remote programmers aren't strangers to working from public locations, but pair programming from these places can be problematic. Ports may be blocked, incoming traffic cannot be forwarded to your machine, and your connection may not be secure. We could log into a remote machine we share with our pairing partner, but we would lose all of our development tools, dotfiles, and other local configuration. Instead, we'll solve these problem by routing our traffic through a virtual cloud server.

A virtual cloud server is one of the most important tools a remote programmer can have. Virtualization in the cloud is so mature that we can quickly and easily do anything remotely that we can do locally. We'll use our virtual server to solve many kinds of problems—including the common problem of getting a good connection at a coffee shop.

We'll begin by creating an Amazon EC2 instance, and setting it up to act as a reverse proxy. A reverse proxy can connect two development machines without our reconfiguring a network router or firewall. We'll reroute the SSH connection we created in the previous chapter through this tunnel and continue sharing a tmux session. We'll also route our web traffic through the proxy, and finally we'll install tmate on the server to make the process easier. Later in the book, we'll repurpose our proxy server for a variety of other jobs.

Let's create the server.

Creating a Reverse Proxy Server

A proxy server is a computer (either virtual or physical) that sits in between two computers communicating with each other, as the following figure shows.

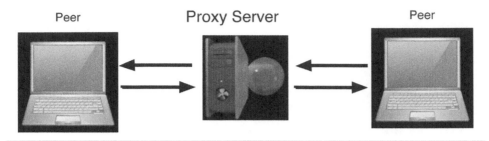

Figure 10—A proxy server forwards traffic between two endpoints.

There are many reasons for using a proxy, depending on the application. A proxy that forwards requests unmodified is called a *gateway* or a *tunnel*, and it may serve to hide one endpoint from the other. In other scenarios it may filter or throttle requests. The following figure illustrates the kind of proxy we'll use, a *reverse* proxy.

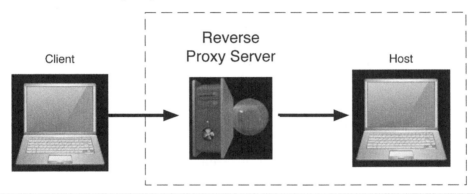

Figure 11—A reverse proxy forwards incoming requests to an endpoint.

With a reverse proxy scenario, the proxy server appears to clients as an ordinary server, but the requests it receives are forwarded to another computer. The responses to those requests are returned to the client as if they came directly from the proxy.

The advantage of using a reverse proxy is that the host's connection to the proxy is established locally (that is, you run a command on your computer to create the connection), which saves us from having to reconfigure a router to handle port forwarding and such. And because the proxy is outside of the local network, a client can easily access it from the Internet at large. This level of availability is the most essential characteristic of a proxy used for pairing, and that's why we'll use the highly available Amazon EC2 platform to host our server.

The server won't do any heavy lifting—it's a tunnel. It forwards to our machine the network traffic it receives. For that reason, the least powerful tier of EC2 servers will be sufficient for us. These *microinstances*, as they are called, are free for the first twelve months. Let's create one.

Open a browser and navigate to the Amazon Web Services (AWS) site.[1] Create an account, and then browse to the AWS Console page.[2] Select the EC2 option from that page and, on the next page, select the Launch Instance button under the Create Instance section, as the following figure shows.

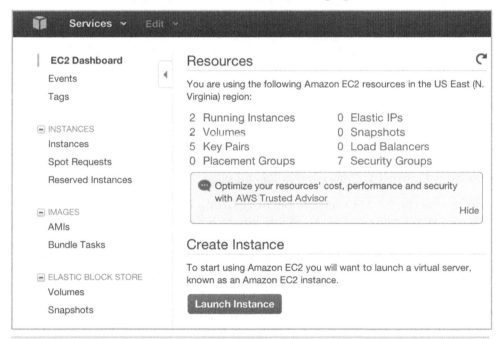

Figure 12—The EC2 dashboard with its Launch Instance button

In the page that opens, select the check box next to the Free Tier Only option. Then scroll down and select the 64-Bit Ubuntu Server 12.04.2 LTS option by pressing the Select button (see Figure 13, *The EC2 quick-launch page*, on page 30).

On the next three pages, press the Next button. We'll eventually reach a page titled Step 5: Tag Instance. This is where we'll name our instance. In the

---

1.   http://aws.amazon.com
2.   https://console.aws.amazon.com

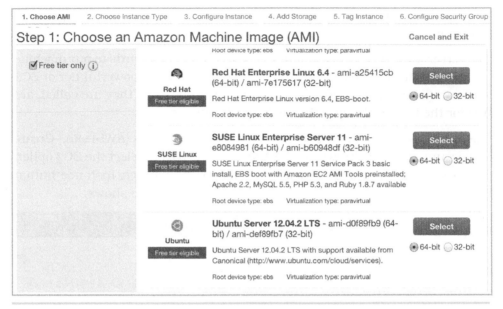

Figure 13—The EC2 quick-launch page

Value field next to the prepopulated Key field, enter the value sharing-proxy, as shown in Figure 14, *Entering a value*, on page 31.

Then press the Next: Configure Security Group button, which will take us to the security settings page. Here, we must create a new custom TCP rule to allow traffic on the port we want to tunnel through. Press the Add Rule button, and a new row will appear in the table. From the Protocol drop-down menu, choose Custom TCP Rule. In the Port Range field, enter 5900. In the Source drop-down menu, choose Anywhere, which will populate the field next to it with 0.0.0.0/0. Your security configuration should now look like Figure 15, *Adding a TCP rule to the EC2 instance*, on page 31.

Press the Review and Launch button, which will take us to a page titled Step 7: Review Instance Launch. Press the Launch button, and a dialog will appear prompting us to choose an existing key pair or create a new key pair. From the first drop-down menu in this dialog, select Create a New Key Pair. In the text field below it, enter the value amazon, as Figure 16, *Creating a new EC2 key pair*, on page 32 shows.

Press the Download Key Pair button to download the key-pair file, which will be named amazon.pem. Put the file in your ~/.ssh directory. We'll user it later when we connect to the server.

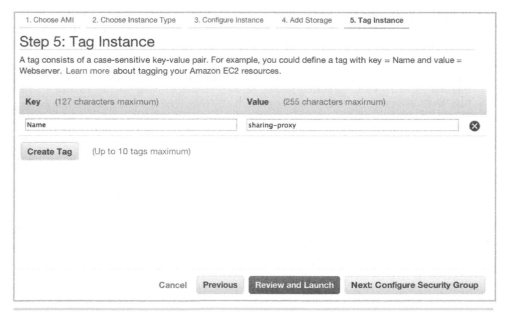

Figure 14—Entering a value

Figure 15—Adding a TCP rule to the EC2 instance

Finally, press the Launch Instances button. It will take us to a status page that confirms our instance has been created. At the bottom of the page is a View Instances button. Click it to see the dashboard page, where our new

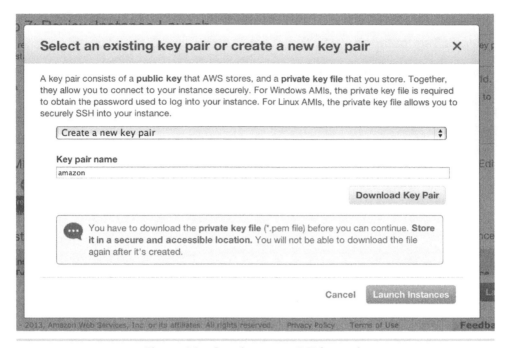

Figure 16—Creating a new EC2 key pair

sharing-proxy instance is listed. One of the columns in the dashboard will be titled Instance State. Ensure the instance achieves a running value in this column.

Select the instance by clicking on the row in the dashboard table. Its details will be displayed in a pane at the bottom of the dashboard. We'll see the public DNS name for our instance among these details, and it will look something like ec2-0-0-0-0.compute-1.amazonaws.com. Make note of this name—we'll need it in the next step.

Now we'll log into the EC2 instance and change some of its SSH configuration. Run the following command to connect to it, but replace the host name with the DNS name you noted a moment ago.

```
$ ssh -i ~/.ssh/amazon.pem ubuntu@ec2-0-0-0-0.compute-1.amazonaws.com
```

After accepting the RSA key for the server, we'll see a prompt like the following.

```
ubuntu@domU-0-0-0-0:~$
```

From here, we need to enable gateway ports so the SSH server will listen for our forwarded port on the machine's public IP address—by default it will listen only on the loopback address. We do this in the /etc/ssh/sshd_config file by adding the following line to it.

```
GatewayPorts yes
```

We can do this by running one command.

```
ubuntu@domU-0-0-0-0:~$ sudo sed -i '1iGatewayPorts yes' \
> /etc/ssh/sshd_config
```

Now we need to restart the SSH process so that it picks up our new configuration. Run this command:

```
ubuntu@domU-0-0-0-0:~$ sudo service ssh restart
ssh stop/waiting
ssh start/running, process 19891
```

When the command is complete, we're ready to use the server as a proxy.

Creating the Secure Tunnel

Our EC2 instance is all set up, but it's not a proxy yet. We can turn it into a proxy by running the following command with the amazonaws.com address replaced by the server's DNS name:

```
$ ssh -R *:5900:localhost:22 -i ~/.ssh/amazon.pem \
> ubuntu@ec2-0-0-0-0.compute-1.amazonaws.com -N
```

The -R option tells the ssh command to create a reverse tunnel (that is, the traffic received by the proxy will be forwarded to the machine that ran the ssh command). The *:5900:localhost:22 argument, which is passed to the -R flag, instructs the command to map port 5900 on the proxy to port 22 on localhost (that is, the computer from which we ran the ssh command). We've chosen to use 5900 because it is a common port for tools like VNC, but it will work equally well for SSH and tmux.

The -i ~/.ssh/amazon.pem ubuntu@ec2-0-0-0-0.compute-1.amazonaws.com option is the standard way of connecting to an EC2 instance using the .pem file we downloaded earlier. Finally, the -N option tells the command not to bring up a terminal session for the remote machine (the EC2 instance). We could also add -f if we want it to run in the background.

Now we can connect an SSH client to the EC2 proxy just as if we were connecting directly to the host machine. Let's simulate this by connecting with two users, bill and ted. You can create these accounts, or follow along with any two users on your machine.

First, hide the terminal that's running the reverse proxy. Then open a second terminal, switch to the ted user, and start a tmux session like this:

```
ted@localhost$ tmux -S /var/tmux/pair
```

Now open a third terminal, switch to the bill user, and execute the following command. When prompted, use the password for bill on localhost instead of the password for ec2-0-0-0-0.compute-1.amazonaws.com:

```
bill@localhost$ ssh -p 5900 ec2-0-0-0-0.compute-1.amazonaws.com
The authenticity of host '[ec2-0-0-0-0.compute-1.amazonaws.com]:5900 ...
RSA key fingerprint is 96:af:b5:c3:d2:61:95:fc:b1:5a:85:32:09:a6:9c:a2.
Are you sure you want to continue connecting (yes/no)? yes
Warning: Permanently added '[ec2-0-0-0-0.compute-1.amazonaws.com]:5900 ...
Password:
bill@localhost$
```

We've created an SSH session through the proxy on port 5900, which will be forwarded to the host machine. We don't need to use the .pem file as before because we're not actually connecting to the EC2 instance. Instead, we are connecting to localhost, and the credentials for bill will be sufficient.

Now that we've created our loopback SSH session (via the proxy), we can use tmux as we did in Chapter 2, *Collaborating with Text Only*, on page 11. Run this command:

```
bill@localhost$ tmux -S /var/tmux/pair attach
```

A new tmux session will open and mirror the session in ted's terminal—just as it did in the previous chapter—but the traffic will be tunneled through the EC2 instance.

The beauty of this setup is that it no longer matters where we are. As long as you and your pairing partner can both reach the EC2 instance, you can share a tmux session. But we can use the reverse proxy for more than just tmux. We can use it for transferring a single file with SCP, allowing a remote browser to view a web application running locally, or even sharing our entire screen.

Before we move on, close the tmux sessions but leave the tunnel running. We'll use it to route web traffic from one pairing partner through the network of the other partner.

Tunneling Web Traffic Through a Proxy

Bill and Ted, our pairing partners from the previous section, need to do more than edit code. They also need to execute code and test it from an end-user's perspective. High bandwidth solutions such as screen sharing simplfy this task, but a low bandwidth option exists if Bill and Ted are developing a web application. Bill can access a web server running on Ted's machine as if it were running locally by using a Socket Secure (SOCKS) proxy. This kind of proxy routes web traffic through an SSH tunnel.

We'll create a SOCKS proxy and configure it to use the tunnel we created earlier. Then we'll reroute our web browser traffic through the proxy and gain access to a remote web server. This technique is particularly handy for web application development, but it's also useful in situations where our remote partner has a VPN connection we are not privy to.

The following examples work best when the users bill and ted are represented by two distinct computers. If possible, run the steps for ted on your primary machine and the steps for bill on another machine. The ted user is already running the tunnel we created earlier. From bill's terminal, run the following command, which creates a SOCKS proxy.

```
bill@localhost$ ssh -D 8080 -C -N -p 5900 \
> ec2-0-0-0-0.compute-1.amazonaws.com
```

In conjunction with the tunnel, the SOCKS proxy creates an end-to-end channel for traffic of all kinds. The -D 8080 option instructs the ssh command to forward local traffic on port 8080 through the tunnel. The -C option requests the compression of all data, including images and large javascript files. The -p 5900 option instructs the command to use the port we opened on the EC2 Server.

As before, the -N option tells the command not to bring up a terminal session, and ec2-0-0-0-0.compute-1.amazonaws.com is our cloud server, which you must replace with the address of the server you created. Because we have not included a username with the connection string, the command will attempt to connect as bill because we are currently logged in as bill. However, this requires a bill user be present on the remote machine, which it will if the same machine is used for both sides of the pair. But you may want to replace bill with the tmux user you created in Chapter 2, *Collaborating with Text Only*, on page 11. If so, replace the last argument in the ssh command with tmux@ec2-0-0-0-0.compute-1.amazonaws.com. Then you can use the github-auth Gem to add bill's private key to the tmux account.

Before bill can use the end-to-end channel, we must tell the software on his machine about the SOCKS proxy. For the Firefox browser, on all platforms, we configure this in the Advanced Network settings dialog. On Mac, open Firefox>Preferences>Advanced>Network. On Ubuntu, open Edit>Preferences>Advanced>Network. And on Windows, open Tools>Options>Advanced>Network.

On any platform, select the "Settings…" button from the Connection section as shown in the following figure.

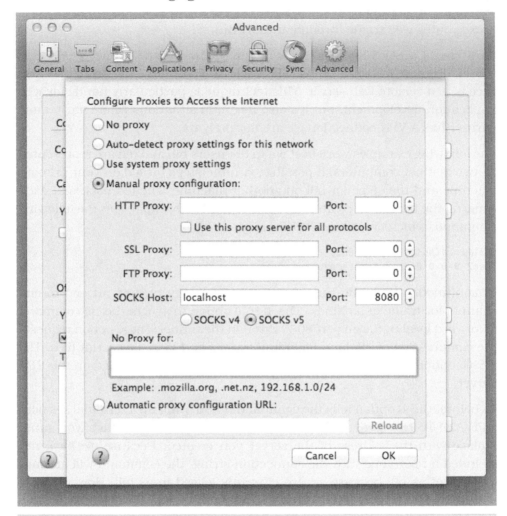

Figure 17—The Firefox proxy settings dialog

Select "Manual Proxy Configuration" and enter localhost for the SOCKS host and 8080 for the port. Then remove the localhost and 127.0.0.1 entires from the "No Proxy for:" field so it is empty.

For other browsers and platforms, this will be set in different ways. On Linux, most applications will obey the SOCKS_PROXY environment variable. On Mac, it can be set globally in the System Preferences>Network>Advanced>Proxies dialog.

Let's test our proxy. In Firefox, browse to http://www.whatsmyip.org/ or any other website that will display the IP address we are accessing it from. We'll find the address it displays is the address of the remote computer we are tunneled through (that is, ted's computer). If you are running this example with a single computer and the IP addresses for bill and ted are the same, you can simulate the experiment by tunneling through the EC2 server only. Replace port 5900 in the command above with 22, and the username with ubuntu. You'll find the website displays the address of the EC2 server instead of your own address.

Now we can use Firefox to get the same view of the web as our partner. If ted is connected to a VPN, bill will be able to access the same intranet sites. If ted is running a local web server, bill can browse to it with the same localhost address—even if it's running on a different port.

Before we move on, kill the tunnel and the proxy by pressing Ctrl-c in the terminal window where each is running. In the next section, we'll use a tool that creates its own tunnel.

Simple Tunneling with tmate

Our cloud server, ssh tunneling, and the SOCKS proxy provide a secure, reliable and lightweight means of connecting to another programmer. The skills required to create this environment are essential—especially when sharing a web server—but they can become cumbersome. As a result, most remote developers write custom tools that make the process easier. These tools range from simple shell scripts to complete applications. One such application is tmate, which makes a remote connection easier, faster, and even more secure.

tmate is a fork of tmux that adds a remote connection feature. We create a tmate session much like a tmux session, but the session immediately connects to a slave server in the cloud making it easy for a remote client to access. The communication between the server and the slave uses msgpack to compress the traffic.[3] Compression improves expensive actions like scrolling in Vim, which can generate massive amounts of data.

tmate can coexist with tmux, and it's even intended to run alongside it. Thus, we can begin by installing tmate. Follow instructions for your platform from the tmate website.[4] As with tmux, Windows users must do this from a VM.

With tmate installed, start a new session from ted's terminal by running the following command:

---

3.   http://msgpack.org/
4.   http://tmate.io/

ted@localhost$ **tmate**

When tmate opens, it will look almost exactly like a tmux session. In fact, it will even obey your ~/.tmux.conf file. But at the bottom of the window, you'll notice something different. tmate displays a command we can give to our partner so he or she can connect to us, as show in the following figure. By default, it uses a tmate.io server but we'll reconfigure that in a moment.

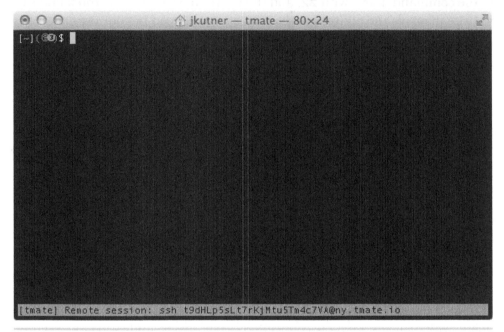

Figure 18—A tmate session

Try to connect from bill's terminal—it will look something like the following command.

bill@localhost$ **ssh bU4P9I5MHyWQE7YvyraahN1xc@ny.tmate.io**

A tmate session will open and bill will be connected to ted's session from across the internet. We can confirm this in ted's window—at the bottom of the screen we'll see a message like this:

[tmate] Your mate has joined the session (51.120.2.94)

bill is not directly connected to ted, though. The tmate-slave server, which is running at ny.tmate.io, is a proxy between the two machines. This service is a courtesy of the tmate developers, and its architecture looks like the following figure.

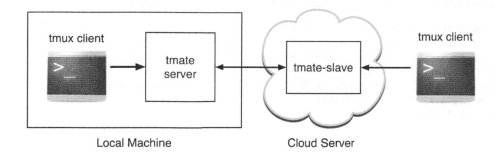

Figure 19—The tmate connection architecture

On ted's machine, which is acting as the local machine, a regular tmux client is attached to a local tmate server. The tmate server runs in a jail, a Linux term for a process that cannot access directories outside of its root directory. It also has its own process ID namespace and lacks any user privileges. These security measures protect against a potential attacker trying to connect to the session.

While the tmate connection architecture is secure and fast, it has the disadvantage of being dependent on the kindness, availability and trustworthiness of the tmate folks (that is, if the tmate-slave is hacked or crashes, you'll have to wait for them to fix it). Fortunately, we can create a tmate-slave of our own, and our EC2 server is the perfect place to host it.

Log into the EC2 server with this command, but use our EC2 host name in place of the amazonaws.com address:

```
$ ssh -i ~/.ssh/amazon.pem ubuntu@ec2-0-0-0-0.compute-1.amazonaws.com
```

Then install the tmate dependencies by running this command:

```
ubuntu@domU-0-0-0-0$ sudo apt-get install git-core build-essential \
> pkg-config libtool libevent-dev libncurses-dev zlib1g-dev automake \
> libssh-dev cmake ruby
```

Next, download the tmate-slave source code and move into the newly created directory by running these commands:

```
ubuntu@domU-0-0-0-0$ git clone https://github.com/nviennot/tmate-slave.git
ubuntu@domU-0-0-0-0$ cd tmate-slave/
```

Now we must create some security keys that tmate will use to authenticate itself. Run this command:

```
ubuntu@domU-0-0-0-0$ ./create_keys.sh
```

The output contains three keys that look like the following

```
Generating public/private dsa key pair.
Your identification has been saved in keys/ssh_host_dsa_key.
Your public key has been saved in keys/ssh_host_dsa_key.pub.
The key fingerprint is:
99:6f:20:fb:93:c1:75:ec:82:57:3c:af:cd:76:1e:d8 ubuntu@domU-0-0-0-0-0-0
The key's randomart image is:
+--[ DSA 1024]----+
|                 |
|                 |
|          o      |
|        o. *     |
|       ..So + o  |
|       o+oo . +  |
|      . +o. = E  |
|       .o.  . + o|
|        ..   . o.|
+-----------------+
```

The first key, shown here, is a DSA key. The other two are RSA and ECDSA keys. The important part is the long colons delimited string, which is 99:6f:20:fb:93:c1:75:ec:82:57:3c:af:cd:76:1e:d8 in the preceding example. Make note of these three keys—we will need them in a moment.

Next, compile the tmate-slave source, which may take some time, like so:

ubuntu@domU-0-0-0-0$ **./autogen.sh && ./configure && make**

Finally, start the tmate-slave on port 5899 by running the following command (as always, replace the amazonaws.com host name with the name of our server):

ubuntu@domU-0-0-0-0$ **sudo ./tmate-slave **
> -p 5900 -h ec2-0-0-0-0.compute-1.amazonaws.com

Leave that process running, and return to your local machine with ted's terminal. We'll configure tmate to connect to this slave instead of tmate.io. Create a ~/.tmate.conf file and add the following code to it:

```
set -g tmate-server-host "ec2-0-0-0-0.compute-1.amazonaws.com"
set -g tmate-server-port 5900
set -g tmate-server-dsa-fingerprint   "f5:26:31:c3:8a:78:6e:5c:77:74:0f:..."
set -g tmate-server-rsa-fingerprint   "af:2d:81:c1:fe:49:70:2d:7f:09:a9:..."
set -g tmate-server-ecdsa-fingerprint "c7:a1:51:36:d2:bb:35:4b:0a:1a:c0:..."
set -g tmate-identity ""
```

Replace the tmate-server-host value with the name of your EC2 server, and replace each of the three keys with the key string you noted earlier.

Now, when we create a new tmate session it will pick up our configuration file. Run the tmate command from ted's terminal like so:

```
ted@localhost$ tmate
```

At the bottom of the window, we see the "Remote session" string again, but it will contain an amazonaws.com address instead of the tmate.io address. Run the command in bill's terminal. It will look something like this:

```
bill@localhost$ ssh -p5900 \
> nc3ojglTpXT586k3UNA50tHGE@ec2-0-0-0-0.compute-1.amazonaws.com
```

bill and ted are now connected through the tmate-slave, which is functioning as a proxy for the session.

Hosting the tmate-slave on our EC2 server has the advantage of being more secure because we can control its access and protect it from being hacked. We could even host the tmate-slave behind a firewall if we were very paranoid. It is also more reliable. If the slave crashes, we can easily restart it without any assistance from a third party. We can even change its location on a whim.

The disadvantage of using tmate is that it forks tmux. As a result, it may lag behind the future progress of the tmux source code. tmux is very stable, but tmate is very much in its infancy.

Choosing between traditional tmux and the very new tmate is probably an organizational decision. In either case, a cloud server should be an essential part the connection architecture. As our remote pairing environment evolves, the importance of this server will grow. In the next chapter, we'll use this server to handle more robust kinds of traffic.

What's Next?

Yogi Berra once said, "In theory, practice and theory are the same. In practice, they aren't." Many remote pair programming techniques are simple in theory, but in practice we have to deal with the fact that you and your pairing partner will connect across two different networks—a task that is often nontrivial.

The virtual cloud server we've created in this chapter is a big step toward solving the real-world problems of remote pair programming. It's one of the most important tools a remote pair programmer can have, but there are many other ways we can create it. Here are some additional tools you might want to try:

ngrok[5] This free service lets you create a tunnel from a public Internet address to a port on your local machine. You can share this URL to give anyone access to a service running on your development machine. Advanced features, such as password protection and custom domains, require a paid subscription.

Linode[6] Many developers use this popular virtual private server host as an alternative to Amazon EC2 for small, cloud-based virtual machines. It supports most flavors of Linux, but not Windows.

prgmr.com[7] Another EC2 alternative. It emphasizes support for programmers with its slogan, "We don't assume you are stupid." prgmr.com gives you unrestricted root access and lets you install your own Linux kernel.

DigitalOcean[8] This cloud hosting platform is similar to Linode. It supports Linux but not Windows. DigitalOcean provides all users with high-performance solid-state drives in instances called *droplets*. The company claims to be able to provision a new droplet within fifty-five seconds.

Dynamic DNS Instead of using a cloud server as a reverse proxy, we could have set up a Dynamic DNS that would allow us to access a machine directly even if the IP address were to change (as is common with home Internet service providers, and inevitable when moving to a coffee shop). One example of this kind of service is DynDNS.[9]

There are endless possibilities for what we can do with these technologies. A virtual cloud server can act as a reverse proxy, as we've seen, but it can also host a browser or even an entire programming environment. In the next chapter you'll learn about some new methods for pair programming, and we'll use our EC2 instance to facilitate them. You'll learn how to use it to share an entire screen or just a single window.

---

5. https://ngrok.com/
6. https://www.linode.com
7. http://prgmr.com/xen/
8. https://www.digitalocean.com/
9. http://dyn.com/dns/dyndns-pro/

CHAPTER 4

Collaborating with Shared Screens

The terminal-based environment we've created is great, but it won't help us view a mobile device emulator, debug JavaScript in a browser, tweak web-page layouts using CSS, or design application graphics. Many pair-programming tasks are possible only when viewing your partner's screen, and unless your application only interfaces with other software, those tasks are unavoidable.

Despite the essential role of screen sharing in pair programming, many developers dread it because of the terrible latency and high bandwidth requirements of most clients. But you'll learn how to use techniques that are responsive, consume very little bandwidth, work on all platforms, and still allow for two-way control.

That's not to say we should get rid of the terminal-based environment. Many programmers use tmux in conjunction with screen sharing. Ultimately, no matter what platform we use or what kind of application we're building, at some point we will need to share our screen. Let's discuss how to do it.

Choosing a Screen-Sharing Tool

Screen sharing is so easy that your boss can probably do it. In fact, management types do it all the time with products like WebEx and Live Meeting. But those tools aren't best for pair programming because they don't allow for two-way control.

There are, however, many other kinds of screen-sharing applications. In fact, there are three other categories, all useful in their own way.

Lowest Common Denominator   This category is characterized by ubiquity. Virtual Network Computing (VNC), Remote Desktop Protocol, and the Mac app Screen Sharing (built upon VNC) are the lowest common denominators of screen-sharing technologies because they're often packaged with a computer's operating system. However, they lack many powerful features. They also require high-bandwidth, low-latency connections because they share an entire screen—not just the parts in use.

Commercial There are many high-quality commercial screen-sharing applications on the market. The most popular for pair programmers are Screenhero, join.me, and TeamViewer.[1,2,3] Although these tools work very well and have a good reputation, they are not perfect and some are expensive.

The Next Generation This category includes tools that use the Next Generation X Window System (NX), which lets two users share an X Window session. It was developed by NoMachine, an Italian software company, but there are many free and open source implementations of the protocol. The NX technology is much faster than VNC and has better security and display quality.

We'll focus on VNC and NX in this chapter because they are the best options for pair programming. Although NX is a superior technology, VNC's ubiquity and cross-platform support make it an essential tool for your pair-programming quiver.

Using VNC for Complete Screen Sharing

Imagine that we're pair-programming on an iPhone application. We may be using tmux and a reverse proxy to share code with our partner, but eventually we'll need to run our app in the simulator. When we start encountering bugs, we may even want to share Xcode (an integrated development environment for developing iOS and Mac applications), and Instruments (a performance- and behavior-analysis tool).[4] The same would apply for respective Android technologies.

For this kind of advanced pairing, few options are better than the Mac's built-in Screen Sharing app, which is built on VNC. Even if you aren't using a Mac, you can connect to one with other VNC clients. In fact, that's exactly what developers at many major iPhone development shops use.[5] But even if we aren't doing iOS work, we'll still need VNC for a variety of pair-programming tasks. Let's set it up.

---

1. http://screenhero.com/
2. https://join.me/
3. http://www.teamviewer.com/en/index.aspx
    4. https://developer.apple.com/technologies/tools/
    5. http://pivotallabs.com/how-we-use-tmux-for-remote-pair-programming/

You'll need a second computer to follow along with the examples in this section. It will act as the client that views our shared screen. We'll refer to our original computer as the server, and the second computer as the client.

We need to set up a VNC-based screen-sharing application on both the client and server. If you're running Mac OS X, then your best option is the built-in app called Screen Sharing. It's capable of detecting and preserving Mac-specific settings like tap-to-click, and multifinger gestures such as two-finger scrolling. Hands down, it is the best option for screen sharing on the Mac.

On the server, if it's a Mac, open System Preferences and select Sharing under the Internet & Wireless section. Then select Screen Sharing from the list on the left, and ensure that the check box next to it is checked. In the right panel, select the radio button next to All Users, as the following figure shows.

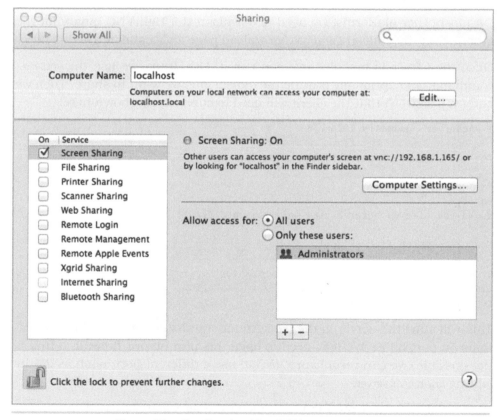

Figure 20—Configuring Mac OS X screen sharing

If you have users on your system who can log in without a password, then you may want to select only users that are secure. For Mac clients, we won't need to do anything—it's already configured for us.

If either the server or the client is not running Mac OS, we need to install a VNC server and viewer, respectively. Any VNC application will do, but we'll use TightVNC, a free and open source option.

On Debian-based Linux systems like Ubuntu, we can install the TightVNC server like this:

```
$ apt-get install tightvncserver
```

And we can install the viewer like this:

```
$ apt-get install xtightvncviewer
```

On most other platforms, we need to download the TightVNC binary for the system from the official TightVNC download page and install it. Do this now.[6]

Once the server is installed, we can run it. On Linux, we use the vncserver command, and optionally provide the dimensions we want to share. Then we enter a password that the client will need to connect, as shown here:

```
$ vncserver -geometry 1024x768

You will require a password to access your desktops.

Password:
Verify:
Would you like to enter a view-only password (y/n)? n

New 'X' desktop is desktop:1

Creating default startup script ~/.vnc/xstartup
Starting applications specified in ~/.vnc/xstartup
Log file is ~/.vnc/desktop:1.log
```

This will start the server in the background and listen for incoming connections on port 5900. We may need to open this port on our firewall. If that is not possible, we can reconfigure VNC to use a different port, such as 22, by editing /usr/bin/vncserver.

Next, we'll initiate a reverse proxy using the server we created in chapter Chapter 3, *Using the Cloud to Connect*, on page 27. This time, we'll tunnel our VNC traffic through it so our server will be accessible from anywhere on the Internet. Run the following command, but note the subtle difference in the

---

6.   http://www.tightvnc.com/download.php

arguments. We're going to forward all traffic to port 5900 on localhost, which is the port VNC and Mac Screen Sharing use. Run this command, but replace the amazonaws.com address with the name of the EC2 host.

```
$ ssh -R *:5900:localhost:5900 -i ~/.ssh/amazon.pem \
> ubuntu@ec2-0-0-0-0.compute-1.amazonaws.com -N
```

After we run this command, the tunnel is initiated and we can connect a client to it. If the client is a Mac, open the Screen Sharing app with the following command:

```
$ open /System/Library/CoreServices/Screen\ Sharing.app
```

We'll be prompted for a host. Enter the DNS name of the EC2 instance and press *Connect*. Then we'll be asked to provide a username and password. Enter the credentials you would use to physically log into the server. A window will open with the complete contents of the server's screen. Note that not all versions of the Screen Sharing app are compatible with all versions of TightVNC. You may need to install a Mac-specific VNC client, such as Chicken of the VNC,[7] for this to work.

If the client is running Linux, we execute this command:

```
$ vncviewer ec2-0-0-0-0.compute-1.amazonaws.com:5900
```

On Windows, we can open the client application and enter the host name in the graphical user interface, as the following figure shows.

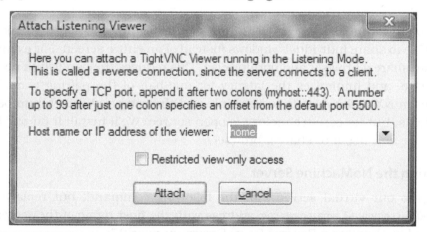

Figure 21—Attaching a Windows VNC client

---

7. http://sourceforge.net/projects/cotvnc/

Now we're ready to do some pair programming with these two machines. Because of the reverse proxy, we can share screens between them no matter what network they're on.

Unfortunately, there are some disadvantages to VNC screen sharing. Large screen resolutions can make the connection's latency unbearable. Most hosts will want to unplug their 30-inch monitors before attempting to use this technique. It's also unlikely that this method will work well from a hotel room or coffee shop.

Another problem with VNC screen sharing is that the host will be more familiar with the development environment than the client will. This can create a good environment for learning, but that may not be of value when the pair is evenly matched.

We'll solve two of these problems by sharing a neutral screen—the screen of the virtual machine we're using as a proxy.

Using NX for Partial Screen Sharing

iOS programming is a unique example because many of the tools needed to run an iOS application work only on a Mac. But now imagine that we're developing a web application. The interface, a browser, can be run on just about any platform. It can even be run on a virtual machine in the cloud and shared equally with both pairing partners. That's exactly what we'll do in this section.

We could do the sharing via VNC, but a better solution is NX. NX makes it possible to share individual windows instead of an entire screen. For example, we can share a browser and nothing else. This reduces the bandwidth needed to share, and minimizes the latency for one-half of the pairing team. The leader in NX technology is NoMachine, and the company sells a number of products, but its core technology is open source. We'll install it on our EC2 instance and use it to share a browser.

Starting the NoMachine Server

Log into our virtual server with the following command, but replace the ec2-0-0-0-0.compute-1.amazonaws.com address with the host name of the server we created in *Creating a Reverse Proxy Server*, on page 27:

```
$ ssh -i ~/.ssh/amazon.pem ubuntu@ec2-0-0-0-0.compute-1.amazonaws.com
```

We see the ubuntu@domU-0-0-0-0:~$ prompt again, but we'll represent it here as $ for the sake of brevity.

Since our goal is to share a browser, we'll begin by installing Firefox. Run this command now:

```
$ sudo apt-get install firefox
```

Next download the NoMachine packages for the NX server, client, and node. The node is a sort of core library for the others. Run these commands:

```
$ wget http://64.34.173.142/download/3.5.0/Linux/nxclient_3.5.0-7_amd64.deb
$ wget http://64.34.173.142/download/3.5.0/Linux/nxnode_3.5.0-9_amd64.deb
$ wget http://64.34.173.142/download/3.5.0/Linux/FE/nxserver_3.5.0-11_amd64.deb
```

Now install those packages by running this command:

```
$ sudo dpkg -i nxnode_3.5.0-3_i386.deb nxserver_3.5.0-4_i386.deb \
> nxclient_3.5.0-7_i386.deb
```

To use the NX server, we need to make some adjustments to our SSH settings. They must allow us to connect to the server with a password instead of the .pem file we used earlier. This is necessary for the NoMachine client. Open the main SSH configuration file with vi by running this command.

```
$ sudo vi /etc/ssh/sshd_config
```

Now find the line containing the text PasswordAuthentication no by pressing / and then typing PasswordAuthentication . As you type, the cursor will be moved to the proper location. Once it's there, press Return and then dd to delete the line. Then press o to enter editing mode and type these lines:

```
PasswordAuthentication yes
UsePam yes
```

When you've finished typing, press Esc and then type :x to save the file and close Vi.

By default, the *ubuntu* user does not have a password. We must create one by running this command:

```
$ sudo passwd ubuntu
```

Now we can restart the SSH service and it will pick up the new configuration. Run this command:

```
ubuntu@domU-0-0-0-0:~$ sudo service ssh restart
ssh stop/waiting
ssh start/running, process 19891
```

We also need to restart the NoMachine server by running this command:

```
$ sudo /etc/init.d/nxserver restart
```

With the nxserver running we can check that our user is configured properly by running this command:

```
$ sudo /usr/NX/bin/nxserver --usercheck ubuntu
```

We're all set. Let's exit the SSH session and connect an NX client to our server.

Connecting a NoMachine Client

Download the NoMachine client software for your platform from the NoMachine website.[8] The Player (the client application) and the server may be bundled together in a single distribution.

When we open the NoMachine Player application, we'll see a dashboard page like the one shown in Figure 22, *The NoMachine Player dashboard*, on page 50. Click New Connection, and a form like the one shown in Figure 23, *Creating a new NoMachine connection*, on page 51, will appear. Name the connection *ec2* and enter the host name of our EC2 instance in the Host field. Then select the radio button for Use NoMachine Login. We'll use the default NoMachine key when authenticating against the NoMachine server.

Figure 22—The NoMachine Player dashboard

---

8.   http://www.nomachine.com/download.php

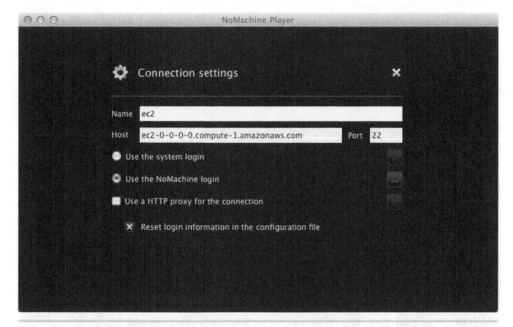

Figure 23—Creating a new NoMachine connection

The NoMachine server and Player ship with a default key that will always be accepted. This means our connection will be encrypted, but not very secure. However, because we're connecting over an SSH channel we don't have to worry much. Alternatively, we can create our own keys and register them with both the server and clients.

Click the X on the connection form, and return to the dashboard. Our new ec2 connection will be listed at the bottom. When we select it, the Player connects to our EC2 server, but we won't get far before it asks for our username and password. Enter ubuntu and the password we set earlier. Then click the OK button.

Now that we've connected to the NoMachine server we need to create a session. This is not very different from the concept of tmux sessions. Click the Create a New Session link from the server-management page, and you'll see a list of options like those shown in Figure 24, *Creating a new NoMachine session*, on page 52. Most of these options are for creating a session with a complete desktop environment like Gnome or KDE. But that's actually what we're trying to avoid. Scroll down the list until you see Create a New Custom Session and select it.

In the custom session form that opens, select the radio button next to Run the Following Command. Then enter firefox in the text field next to that, and check the box next to Run the Command in a Virtual Desktop, as Figure 25, *Creating a new NoMachine session with a custom command*, on page 52 shows. Then click the OK button.

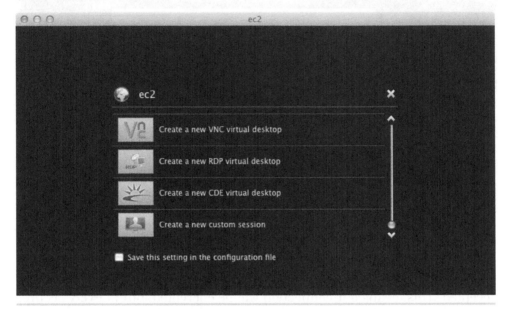

Figure 24—Creating a new NoMachine session

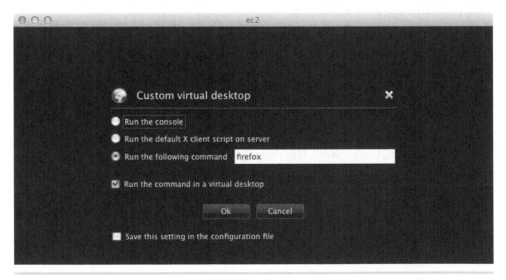

Figure 25—Creating a new NoMachine session with a custom command

After a short while and a splash screen that must be closed, we'll see the Firefox browser running inside of the NoMachine Player, as the following figure shows. This browser is running on the EC2 instance, and any other NoMachine Player client that can connect to the same server can also take part in this browser session. If you have a second computer, try it out now.

Figure 26—Firefox running in a NoMachine session

We can point this browser to any location on the Internet. If we're running a reverse proxy for a web server running on our local machine, we can use this browser to access it, and both pairing partners will see the same thing.

But what if we took it one step further? What if this browser didn't need to make a round-trip? What if it could hit a web server running right on the same EC2 instance it's running on? That's what we'll do in the next chapter.

What's Next?

You've learned about some excellent sharing technologies in this chapter, but you've also learned about a new technique for pairing. Full-screen sharing is an essential tool when you're working from a remote location, because it can solve many collaboration problems that terminal-based tools like tmux can't handle. But many other tools, besides VNC and NX, facilitate screen sharing. Depending on your environment, you may want to try these:

Xpra[9] A free and open source application that allows you to run X Windows programs on a remote host and direct their display to your local machine.

Neatx[10] An open source NX server that is similar to the commercial NX server from NoMachine. It was originally developed by Google and was released as open source in 2009.

We're going in the right direction by using the cloud server to help with the problem of sharing visual assets, but we can go further. In the next chapter you'll learn how to decentralize your pairing environment by using the EC2 instance as more than just a proxy. We can use the server to host the entire pairing session.

---

9.   http://xpra.org/
10. https://code.google.com/p/neatx/

CHAPTER 5

Building a Pairing Server

In this chapter, we'll use Fulcrum,[1] a free open source agile project-planning tool, as the code base for our pairing session. Fulcrum is a complete web application with a front end, a back end, and even a database. As a result, we'll create a more complex development environment than the JavaScript setup we used for Backbone.js in Chapter 2, *Collaborating with Text Only*, on page 11. However, we'll use the same pair-programming tools by deploying this development environment to a new platform.

The best pair-programming environment is secure, accessible, and responsive and gives both parties equal control. The cloud server we used as a reverse proxy in Chapter 3, *Using the Cloud to Connect*, on page 27, improved our ability to connect to a pairing partner, but it did not fix all of our security and connectivity problems. In fact, the extra layer of routing may even have degraded latency and caused a sluggish experience for our remote partner.

For these reasons, we'll repurpose the cloud server and use it as a complete development environment. We'll provision it with our development tools, our application infrastructure, and even our application's source code. We'll create some scripts that set up the programming environment for Fulcrum so we can quickly and easily stand up new environments solely for the purpose of a single pair-programming session.

Initializing the Pairing Server with Vagrant

A pairing server is a centralized environment that is equally accessible by both halves of a pair-programming team. The pairing server contains all of the source code that the pair is working on, as well as the tools needed to run the code.

---

1. http://wholemeal.co.nz/projects/fulcrum.html

In most cases, the pairing server will be hosted in the cloud, but we'll start by building a local virtual machine that's managed by Vagrant. Vagrant uses Oracle's VirtualBox to build configurable, lightweight, and portable virtual machines dynamically.[2] Once we work out the details, we'll deploy our provisioning scripts to the EC2 instance. Because both virtual machines can use the same Ubuntu operating system, the scripts will transfer without difficulty.

You installed Vagrant in the *Preface*, on page ix, so let's open a terminal and run this command to make sure it's healthy:

```
$ vagrant --version
Vagrant version 1.2.3
```

Now run the following commands to create a project directory and initialize the Vagrant configuration for our server.

```
$ mkdir ~/pairing-server
$ cd ~/pairing-server
$ vagrant init pairing-server http://files.vagrantup.com/precise32.box
A `Vagrantfile` has been placed in this directory. You are now
ready to `vagrant up` your first virtual environment! Please read
the comments in the Vagrantfile as well as documentation on
`vagrantup.com` for more information on using Vagrant.
```

The Vagrantfile tells Vagrant the name of the virtual machine we want to interact with when we use the vagrant command. It also defines the URL of the image we'll create our server from. We used the 32-bit Ubuntu Precise (version 12.04).

Next, we need to add some extra configuration that will allow us to access a web server running inside of the virtual machine. Open the Vagrantfile and put this code inside the Vagrant::configure("2") block (you can delete all of the comments in it, but leave the config.vm.box and config.vm.box_url settings):

pairing-server/Vagrantfile
```
config.vm.network :forwarded_port, host: 3000, guest: 3000
```

This will route port 3000 on the virtual machine to port 3000 on the host.

Now we'll boot our virtual machine. Run this command, but be aware that the first time will take a while as Vagrant downloads the precise32.box image:

```
$ vagrant up
Bringing machine 'default' up with 'virtualbox' provider...
[default] Box 'pairing-server' was not found. Fetching box from specified URL for
the provider 'virtualbox'. Note that if the URL does not have
a box for this provider, you should interrupt Vagrant now and add
```

---

2.   https://www.virtualbox.org/

```
the box yourself. Otherwise Vagrant will attempt to download the
full box prior to discovering this error.
Downloading with Vagrant::Downloaders::HTTP...
Downloading box: http://files.vagrantup.com/precise32.box
Extracting box...
Cleaning up downloaded box...
Successfully added box 'pairing-server' with provider 'virtualbox'!
[default] Importing base box 'pairing-server'...
[default] Matching MAC address for NAT networking...
[default] Setting the name of the VM...
[default] Clearing any previously set forwarded ports...
[default] Creating shared folders metadata...
[default] Clearing any previously set network interfaces...
[default] Preparing network interfaces based on configuration...
[default] Forwarding ports...
[default] -- 22 => 2222 (adapter 1)
[default] Booting VM...
[default] Waiting for VM to boot. This can take a few minutes.
[default] VM booted and ready for use!
[default] Configuring and enabling network interfaces...
[default] Mounting shared folders...
[default] -- /vagrant
```

The virtual machine (VM) is running! Let's log in with the following command:

```
$ vagrant ssh
```

This will bring us to a vagrant@precise32:~$ prompt, which means that we are inside the virtual machine as the *vagrant* user. Exit the VM using the exit command, and we'll start creating our provisioning scripts.

Provisioning with Puppet

The pairing server should be easy to destroy and re-create because neither party wants to be responsible for maintaining it or ensuring that all of its software gets upgraded in lockstep with local development environments. That's why an entire development team should maintain provisioning scripts, such as Chef or Puppet scripts, that install the software the pairing server needs when it boots up. These provisioning scripts provide many advantages over manual setup and traditional Shell scripts because they are portable, configurable, and modular, and thus easier to maintain. We'll use Puppet to provision our server because its syntax is declarative and does not require knowledge of any particular programming language.

We need to create a directory for our Puppet scripts on our host machine. Make sure you've exited the VM and run this command from the pairing-server directory:

```
$ mkdir -p puppet/manifests
```

Now create a puppet/manifests/site.pp file to contain our primary configuration. Then add the following code to it.

pairing-server/puppet/manifests/site.pp

```
$username     = "vagrant"
$home         = "/home/${username}"
$app_name     = "fulcrum"
$app_dir      = "${home}/${app_name}"

Exec {
  path => ['/usr/sbin', '/usr/bin', '/usr/local/bin', '/sbin', '/bin']
}
```

This sets up some useful variables and configures the path that Puppet will use when our scripts are running. Now we can add a few resources to the site.pp. They will initialize our server with some essential packages and libraries. Put these lines at the end of the file.

pairing-server/puppet/manifests/site.pp

```
stage { 'preinstall':
  before => Stage['main']
}

class prepare {
  exec { 'apt-get -y update':
    unless => "test -e ${app_dir}"
  }

  package { ['build-essential', 'curl', 'autoconf', 'libgdbm-dev',
    'automake', 'libtool', 'bison', 'pkg-config', 'libffi-dev',
    'libyaml-dev', 'libncurses5-dev', 'libxml2', 'libxml2-dev',
    'libxslt1-dev', 'libqt4-dev', 'postgresql-server-dev-9.1',
    'nodejs', 'libreadline6-dev', 'libssl-dev', 'zlib1g-dev']:
    ensure  => installed,
    require => Exec['apt-get -y update']
  }
}
class { 'prepare':
  stage => preinstall
}
```

This will update our operating system's package manager and download the packages we've defined. It's mostly boilerplate that's necessary to get our image up-to-date and ready for general development work.

Now we must add the site.pp manifest to our Vagrant configuration so it will run when we start up our VM. Open the Vagrantfile and add the following code to the Vagrant::configure("2") block:

```
config.vm.provision :puppet do |puppet|
  puppet.manifests_path = "puppet/manifests"
  puppet.manifest_file = "site.pp"
end
```

Next, we'll tell Vagrant to load and execute the Puppet scripts by running the following command:

```
$ vagrant reload
[default] Attempting graceful shutdown of VM...
[default] Setting the name of the VM...
[default] Clearing any previously set forwarded ports...
[default] Creating shared folders metadata...
[default] Clearing any previously set network interfaces...
[default] Preparing network interfaces based on configuration...
[default] Forwarding ports...
[default] -- 22 => 2222 (adapter 1)
[default] Booting VM...
[default] Waiting for VM to boot. This can take a few minutes.
[default] VM booted and ready for use!
[default] Configuring and enabling network interfaces...
[default] Mounting shared folders...
[default] -- /vagrant
[default] -- /tmp/vagrant-puppet/manifests
[default] -- /tmp/vagrant-puppet/modules-0
[default] Running provisioner: VagrantPlugins::Puppet::Provisioner::Puppet...
Running Puppet with site.pp...
stdin: is not a tty
notice: /Stage[preinstall]/Prepare/Exec[apt-get -y update]/returns: execut...
notice: Finished catalog run in 6.27 seconds
```

Much of the output is similar to the vagrant up command, but Vagrant is also running the provisioner, which loads our Puppet scripts.

Now that our VM has been provisioned with these essentials, we can start adding our development tools.

Installing Development Tools

The tools you'll need for your applications depend on the types of applications you're building. You may need Node.js, Postgres, Hadoop, or any number of other technologies. For our example, we'll install a Ruby runtime, the SQLite database, tmux, and the Xvfb virtual windowing system.

We can include all of these tools in our configuration by adding the following code to the end of the site.pp file.

```
pairing-server/puppet/manifests/site.pp
package { ["ruby1.9.1", "ruby1.9.1-dev", "rubygems1.9.1", "irb1.9.1",
  "libopenssl-ruby1.9.1", "sqlite3", "libsqlite3-dev", "tmux", "xvfb",
  "firefox"]:
    ensure => installed
}
```

We need Xvfb because our pairing server is headless (that is, it has no graphical user interface). But the application we'll be working on is web-based, which means we'll need a browser to run our tests. Xvfb takes the place of a graphical user interface and even a monitor by performing all graphical operations in memory. In this way, our tests can execute in a browser even though the browser won't be rendered on a physical display. This is similar to how we ran the Backbone.js tests on PhantomJS in Chapter 2, *Collaborating with Text Only*, on page 11.

Now we can use the vagrant provision command to run the provisioner and install our new packages:

```
$ vagrant provision
```

With these tools installed, we're ready to work on some code. But first we'll need to get the code.

Installing the Code Base

Our application's source code is stored in a Git repository. As you probably know, Git is a version-control system that tracks changes to a bunch of files. We'll create some Puppet resources to check out the Git repository to our pairing server, and we'll put these resources in a Puppet module. To create the module, run the following command:

```
$ mkdir -p puppet/modules/git/manifests
```

Then add this line of code to the config.vm.provision block in our Vagrantfile so that the provisioner will know where to find our modules the next time it runs.

```
pairing-server/Vagrantfile
puppet.module_path = "puppet/modules"
```

In the puppet/modules/git/manifests directory, create an init.pp file, and add the following code to it:

```
pairing-server/puppet/modules/git/manifests/init.pp
class git {
  package { "git-core":
    ensure => "present"
  }
}
```

This defines a Puppet class named Git that ensures the git-core package is installed. Next, we need to define a function that will allow us to use the git-core package to clone a repository. Add the following code to the end of the file:

pairing-server/puppet/modules/git/manifests/init.pp
```
define git::clone( $path, $source ){
  exec { "git_clone_${name}":
    command => "git clone ${source} ${path}",
    creates => "${path}/.git",
    user => $username,
    require => Package[git-core],
    timeout => 600
  }
}
```

This function takes a $path argument, which is the location where we want to clone the Git repository, and a $source argument, which is the URL of the Git repository we want to clone.

The function body checks to see if the cloned repository already exists (so that we won't repeat the cloning step after restarting the VM). If it doesn't exist, then Puppet will execute the git clone command with our arguments.

Now we can use this function in our Puppet configuration. Open the site.pp file and add the following code to the end of it.

pairing-server/puppet/manifests/site.pp
```
include git
git::clone { $app_name :
  path    => $app_dir,
  source => "git://github.com/malclocke/fulcrum.git"
}
```

This step will vary depending on the location of the application's repository. The application we'll be using, Fulcrum, is hosted on GitHub. However, the repository URL we've specified is a read-only location. That mean's we can't push our commits back to the repository of origin.

In reality, you'll want to commit your code changes and push them to a shared repository. To do this, you'll probably need to provide the Git host with an SSH key. We'll address this later in the chapter when we deploy these Puppet scripts to the cloud.

Let's run vagrant reload again, and have Puppet download Fulcrum's source code.

```
$ vagrant reload
...
[default] Running provisioner: VagrantPlugins::Puppet::Provisioner::Puppet...
Running Puppet with site.pp...
stdin: is not a ttynotice: /Stage[main]/Git/Package[git-core]/ensure: ensure ...
notice: /Stage[main]//Git::Clone[fulcrum]/Exec[git_clone_fulcrum]/returns: ex...
notice: Finished catalog run in 35.90 seconds
```

This time, the provisioner installed Git and cloned the Fulcrum repository.
Now we can initialize the code base, and download any libraries it needs.

Initializing the Code Base

The last few resources we'll add to our configuration are application-specific.
Because Fulcrum is a Ruby on Rails application we must set up some configuration files and run Bundler to download its dependencies. Let's begin with
Bundler. Add the following resource to the end of the site.pp file to ensure that
it's installed.

pairing-server/puppet/manifests/site.pp
```
exec {"install_bundler":
  command => "gem install bundler",
  require => Package['ruby1.9.1', 'rubygems1.9.1']
}
```

The require attribute instructs Puppet to run this resource after installing the
ruby1.9.1 and rubygems1.9.1 packages. Now we can add a resource that uses
Bundler to install our application dependencies. Put this code at the end of
the site.pp file.

pairing-server/puppet/manifests/site.pp
```
exec { "bundle" :
  command => "su ${username} -c 'bundle install'",
  cwd     => $app_dir,
  require => [Git::Clone[$app_name], Exec['install_bundler']]
}
```

The bundle install command will download and install all of the Ruby libraries
that Fulcrum needs. We've also defined the require attribute so this resource
will execute only after the Git repository has been cloned.

Next, we'll create a function that initializes the database for a given environment. Add this code to the end of the site.pp file.

pairing-server/puppet/manifests/site.pp
```
define fulcrum::setup() {
 exec { "fulcrum-setup-${name}":
    command     => "bundle exec rake fulcrum:setup db:setup",
    cwd         => $app_dir,
```

```
    environment => "RAILS_ENV=${name}",
    require     => Exec["bundle"],
    user        => $username
  }
}
```

Now we can invoke this function for the two environments we'll use in our pair-programming work. Add this code to the end of the file:

pairing-server/puppet/manifests/site.pp
```
fulcrum::setup{"development": ;}
fulcrum::setup{"test": ;}
```

Let's run the provisioner one more time so it can run Bundler and download our application's dependencies.

```
$ vagrant provision
[default] Running provisioner: puppet...
Running Puppet with site.pp...
stdin: is not a tty
notice: /Stage[main]//Exec[bundle]/returns: executed successfully
notice: /Stage[main]//Fulcrum::Setup[development]/Exec[fulcrum-setup-develop...
notice: /Stage[main]//Fulcrum::Setup[test]/Exec[fulcrum-setup-test]/returns:...
notice: Finished catalog run in 95.10 seconds
```

Now we're ready to pair-program with our server.

Using the Server

The pairing server will already be up and running once the provisioner is finished. Let's run this command to log into it via SSH as we did earlier in the chapter:

```
$ vagrant ssh
```

Now start a tmux session by running the tmux command. In the new session, change directories to the Fulcrum repository:

```
vagrant@precise32:~$ cd fulcrum
```

Then start the application like this:

```
vagrant@precise32:~/fulcrum$ rails server
```

Now open a browser on the host system and point it to http://localhost:3000. We'll see Fulcrum's login page, as Figure 27, *The Fulcrum login page*, on page 64 shows.

We're ready to start hacking—let's connect a second tmux client.

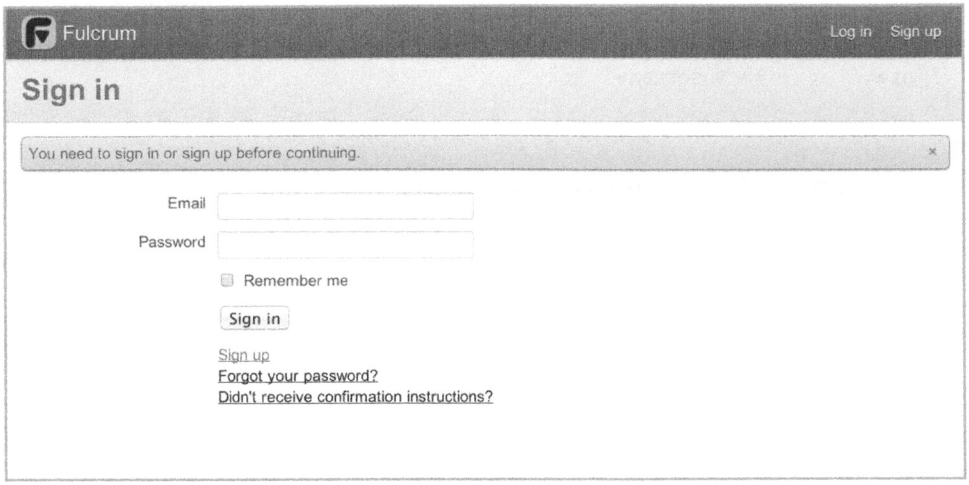

Figure 27—The Fulcrum login page

Open a second terminal window, change to the directory with our Vagrant configuration, and run vagrant ssh. Then run the following command to attach to the tmux session.

```
vagrant@precise32:~$ tmux attach
```

We'll see the same session as in the first terminal. Now we'll explore how two developers might work on this code base.

Split the tmux window into two panes by pressing Ctrl-b %. In the new pane, open one of the application files in an editor by running this command:

```
vagrant@precise32:~/fulcrum$ vi app/models/changeset.rb
```

Now return focus to the first pane (the one running the web server) by pressing Ctrl-b o. Then create a third pane by pressing Ctrl-b " (double quote), which will split the window horizontally. In the new pane, enter the following command to run the unit tests in the context of the Xvfb virtual screen:

```
vagrant@precise32:~/fulcrum$ xvfb-run bundle exec rspec
...........................................................................
...................QFont::setPixelSize: Pixel size <= 0 (0)...................
...........................................................................
.......................................

Finished in 45.44 seconds
234 examples, 0 failures
```

The tests will take a few minutes, and all of them will pass (you might see a few random failures because SQLite doesn't handle database transactions well, but don't worry about those).

In the second terminal session, switch focus to the text editor and type `:5`, which will move the cursor to line five. We'll see this line of code:

```
validates :project, :presence => true
```

Delete the line by typing `dd`. Then save the file by typing `:w`. Return to the pane with the tests and run the same command again:

```
vagrant@precise32:~/fulcrum$ xvfb-run bundle exec rspec
...............................................................
...............QFont::setPixelSize: Pixel size <= 0 (0)............
.............................F..................................
....................................

Failures:

  1) Changeset validations associations must have a valid project
     Failure/Error: changeset.should have(1).errors_on(:project)
       expected 1 errors on :project, got 0
     # ./spec/models/changeset_spec.rb:21:in `block (4 levels) in
       <top (required)>'

Finished in 45.44 seconds
234 examples, 1 failures

Failed examples:

rspec ./spec/models/changeset_spec.rb:19 # Changeset validations
associations must have a valid project
```

A test failed this time. The deleted line in the changeset.rb file is the cause. Let's replace it and fix the test.

In the first terminal session, switch focus back to the text editor and press `u`, which will undo the last change. Change focus to the terminal running the broken test, and run the entire test suite again. All tests will pass.

In this scenario, each of the two terminal sessions represents a pair-programming partner. The process of going back and forth, where one programmer runs the tests and one fixes them, is a common pattern, often called *ping-pong*. We'll discuss this in more detail in Chapter 7, *Remote Pairing in the Wild*, on page 79.

Now we can take this show on the road. Let's deploy this configuration to our EC2 instance.

Running the Server in the Cloud

The Amazon EC2 instance we created and used as a reverse proxy in Chapter 3, *Using the Cloud to Connect*, on page 27, can also make an excellent general-purpose pair-programming environment. It's easily accessible by both parties, and the instances can be stood up and torn down almost as easily as with Vagrant. We can even use the same Puppet scripts.

The scripts we wrote for Vagrant need one little tweak before we can run them in the cloud. Our scripts assume the presence of a *vagrant* user, but on EC2 this will be an *ubuntu* user. To fix this, replace the first line in the site.pp file with this code:

```
pairing-server/puppet/manifests/site.pp
case $::virtual {
  'virtualbox' : {
    $username = "vagrant"
  }
  default : {
    $username = "ubuntu"
  }
}
```

This conditional statement checks the platform the scripts are running on before setting the $username variable. Now we're ready to deploy the scripts to the cloud.

We'll package our puppet scripts into a zip file so we can deploy them in one step. If the zip program is installed on our Mac or Linux systems, we can run this command from the directory with the Vagrant configuration.

```
$ zip -r puppet puppet/
```

If you're on Windows you'll need to open Windows Explorer, locate the puppet directory, right-click, and choose Send To -> Compressed (Zipped) Folder.

Now we can transfer the archive to our EC2 server. Because we already have SSH access, we can do this on Linux and Mac with the scp program by running the following command.

```
$ scp -i ~/.ssh/amazon.pem puppet.zip \
> ubuntu@ec2-0-0-0-0.compute-1.amazonaws.com:~
```

On Windows, you'll need to install WinSCP; download it from the official site and run the executable.[3] You can also use PuTTY and the pscp command with the same arguments shown in the scp command earlier.

---

3. http://winscp.net/eng/index.php

The -i flag, as you'll remember from Chapter 3, *Using the Cloud to Connect*, on page 27, instructs the SSH command to use the amazon.pem key file, which the server uses to authenticate us. Next, we'll log into the EC2 server like this:

```
$ ssh -i ~/.ssh/amazon.pem \
> ubuntu@ec2-0-0-0-0.compute-1.amazonaws.com
```

Now we see the ubuntu@domU-0-0-0-0:~ $ prompt again, which means we're logged into the server.

Cloning the Fulcrum repository doesn't require an SSH key, but if the application you're working on in the future requires one, this would be a good time to create and register it with the server hosting your Git repository. To create the key, run this command, use the default file location, and enter a password.

```
ubuntu@domU-0-0-0-0:~ $ ssh-keygen -t rsa -C "your_email@example.com"
Generating public/private rsa key pair.
Enter file in which to save the key (/home/ubuntu/.ssh/id_rsa): [Press enter]
Enter passphrase (empty for no passphrase): [Type a passphrase]
Enter same passphrase again: [Type passphrase again]
Your identification has been saved in /home/ubuntu/.ssh/id_rsa.
Your public key has been saved in /home/ubuntu/.ssh/id_rsa.pub.
The key fingerprint is:
00:00:00:00:00:00:00:00:00:00:00:00:00:00:00:00 your_email@example.com
```

An id_rsa.pub file was created in the ~/.ssh directory. You can upload this to your Git server. We'll continue without this step because we won't be pushing our changes to the Fulcrum repository.

Next, we'll update the package manager and install two packages needed to run our puppet scripts, like this:

```
ubuntu@domU-0-0-0-0:~ $ sudo apt-get update
ubuntu@domU-0-0-0-0:~ $ sudo apt-get install zip puppet-common
```

The first command updates the local list of package versions, and the second command installs an up-to-date version of the two dependencies. The zip package is a tool for unzipping the puppet.zip file, and puppet-common is the program to run them. We can do the unzipping like so:

```
ubuntu@domU-0-0-0-0:~ $ unzip puppet.zip
```

This creates a puppet directory with the decompressing scripts. Now we must switch to root mode and move into the new directory, like so:

```
ubuntu@domU-0-0-0-0:~ $ sudo -i
root@domU-0-0-0-0:~ $ cd /home/ubuntu/puppet
```

Be careful of the commands you enter in this mode. You can cause a great deal of damage as root. Let's do what we need to do and get out. Enter the following command to run the puppet scripts.

```
root@domU-0-0-0-0:/home/ubuntu/puppet $ puppet apply \
> --modulepath=modules manifests/site.pp
```

Our configuration has been applied, and we can exit root mode.

```
root@domU-0-0-0-0:/home/ubuntu/puppet $ exit
ubuntu@domU-0-0-0-0:~ $
```

We're ready to start pair-programming. All you need to do is create a tmux session, and find a partner to join you.

You probably won't want to run these steps every time you pair with someone. That's why it's helpful to capture an image of this EC2 instance in its current state. You can do this from the EC2 dashboard by selecting your instance, opening the Actions dialog at the top of the screen, and selecting Create Image (EBS AMI). The next time you need a new instance, select Launch Instance and, from the My AMIs tab, choose the image you created.

However, it's perfectly acceptable to leave your pairing server running, or provision it from Puppet scripts each time you start a session. This makes sense if your configuration will change often or if the cost of managing Amazon images is greater than the time it takes to run the Puppet scripts. As with everything else, it depends on the people, processes, and technologies in your organization.

What's Next?

A pairing server is easy to connect to for both parties, it's reproducible, and it's more secure because it eliminates the need for one of the partners to log directly into the other partner's machine.

You won't be sharing a browser, but both partners can point their respective browsers to the same running server. You can even use NX on the pairing server, as you learned in Chapter 4, *Collaborating with Shared Screens*, on page 43, and add its setup to your Puppet scripts. But we'll leave that step as an exercise for you to do on your own.

As with our proxy server, there is nothing unique about Amazon's cloud platform when it comes to building a pairing server. Most of the virtual private server alternatives mentioned in Chapter 3, *Using the Cloud to Connect*, on page 27, can be used to create a pairing server. But there are some other tools that are unique to building this kind of environment:

Packer[4] A tool for creating identical machine images for multiple platforms from a single source configuration. It automates the creation of any type of machine—even Windows. It can be used to build images for platforms including Amazon EC2, DigitalOcean,[5] VirtualBox, and VMware.[6]

Chef[7] Like Puppet, Chef is a configuration-management framework that can be used with Vagrant. The main advantage *and* disadvantage of Chef is that its syntax is based on the Ruby language. This is helpful for developers who already know Ruby, but it often encumbers those who don't.

Unfortunately, most pairing servers limit us to terminal-based editors, which can leave much to be desired for some programmers. In the next chapter, you'll learn how to use a more robust integrated development environment (IDE) for remote pairing.

---

4. http://www.packer.io/
5. https://www.digitalocean.com/
6. http://www.vmware.com/
7. http://www.opscode.com/chef/

CHAPTER 6

Collaborating with an IDE

In one of my favorite pairing experiences I worked alongside a team of Java developers in India. Because I was located in the United States, we had to deal with vastly different time zones and terrible latency. We couldn't find a two-way screen-sharing experience tolerable enough for both parties, and we had trouble sustaining a direct SSH connection. We tried using a virtual cloud server located in the western United States, which was fine for me, but my partner still struggled.

We found a solution to our problem in Eclipse—a development tool we already had in use. The Eclipse integrated development environment (IDE) can be extended by installing various plug-ins that add new behavior.[1] One plug-in, called Saros, enables a collaborative editing environment that works well with high-latency networks.[2]

Saros uses a conflict-resolution algorithm to merge changes from two separate clients, which means two programmers can work on the same file, see the other programmer's changes, and still experience local edit speed (that is, there's no lag for either party after pressing a button or moving the mouse). Saros includes additional collaboration tools such as whiteboarding and instant messaging. It even allows for fine-grained control over what files and directories are shared. In this chapter, you'll learn how to install, configure, and use Saros in your projects—even if they aren't Java projects.

Installing Saros and Eclipse

Eclipse runs on the Java Virtual Machine, which makes it cross-platform-friendly, but it isn't just a tool for Java programmers. We can use Eclipse to

---

1. http://www.eclipse.org/
2. http://www.saros-project.org/

write programs in C/C++, Ruby, Python, Erlang, and many other languages. Eclipse is also free, open source, and extensible, and its feature set can be enhanced by loading plug-ins that add new behavior. It's common to install plug-ins for version-control systems like Git, or static analysis tools like FindBugs and Checkstyle. We'll install the Saros plug-in, which adds the collaborative editing features described earlier.

To properly test Saros, you'll need two computers. If possible, run the steps in this chapter on both machines. But if you have only one computer, continue to follow along, and you'll get a feel for how Eclipse and Saros work. Let's start by installing them.

Download Eclipse from the official download page.[3] Choose the Eclipse Classic 4.2.2 (Juno) package for your platform. Decompress the archive, and run the executable it contains. We'll see the Eclipse launch page (shown in the following figure).

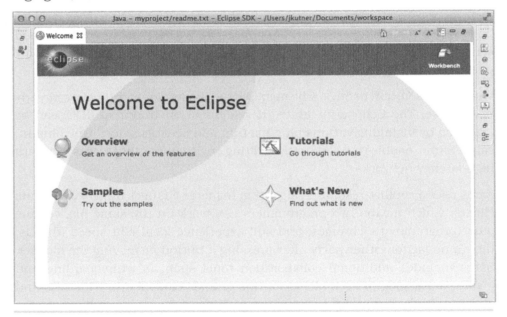

Figure 28—Eclipse welcome page

From the Eclipse menu bar, choose Help -> Install New Software, which opens the Available Software wizard. Select the Add button, and a dialog will prompt us for a name and location. Leave the name blank and enter the URL http://dpp.sourceforge.net/update in the location field. Then press the OK button.

---

3.   http://www.eclipse.org/downloads/

The wizard will download a list of available software, which may take a few minutes. Expand the top node, named DPP, and check the box next to Saros, as the following figure shows.

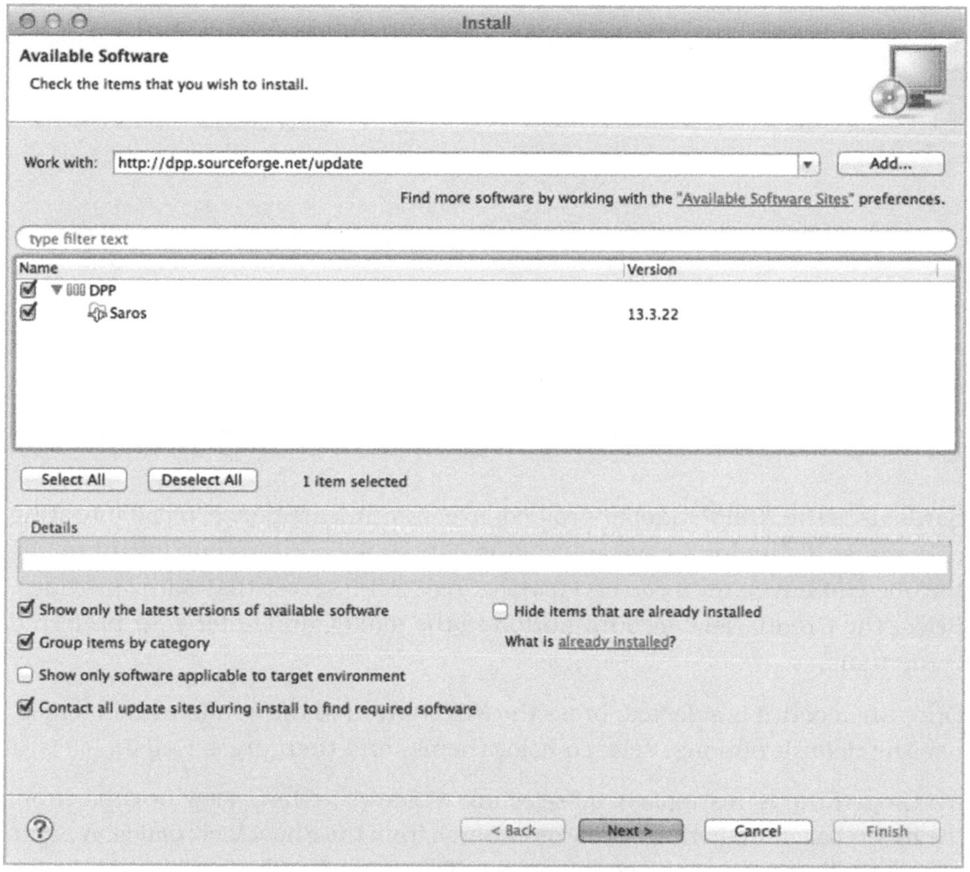

Figure 29—Installing Saros from the Available Software dialog

Press the Next button. Review the items to be installed and press Next again. Then accept the license agreement and press Finish. Finally, restart Eclipse when it asks you to do so.

Now we'll configure Saros. From the menu bar, we see a new Saros option. Select it and then select Start Saros Configuration from the drop-down menu that appears. We need to enter the credentials for an XMPP account, as in Figure 30, *Configuring Saros with an XMPP account*, on page 74.

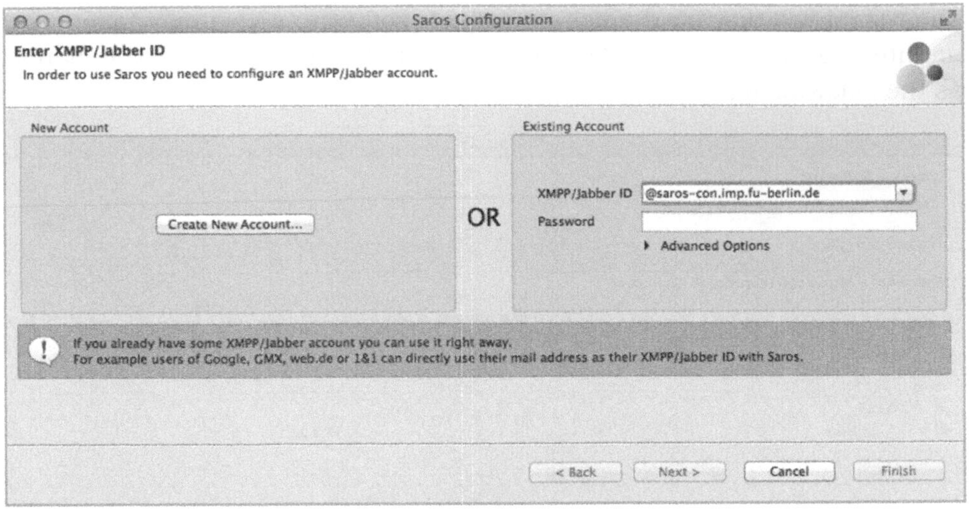

Figure 30—Configuring Saros with an XMPP account

Saros uses the XMPP/Jabber protocol to communicate between collaborating endpoints. If you don't have an existing Jabber account (or don't want to use the one you have), then you can use the free XMPP server that Saros provides. Select the Create New Account button in the dialog, and enter your preferred credentials.

Once an account is selected, press the Next button in the configuration dialog, use the default options, select a color theme, and then press Finish.

Next, open the Saros toolbox by selecting Window -> Show View -> Other from the menu bar, and then select Saros -> Saros from the Show View dialog. A Saros window will appear at the bottom of the IDE. Press the Connect button in the toolbox to make sure your account is connected. Now we're ready to start sharing.

If you're using two computers, then you'll need to set up a different XMPP account on the other computer. If we use the same account it will kick the other instance offline. Do this now. Once we establish two working XMPP connections, we add the second computer as a buddy on the first computer.

Select the Add Buddies option from the Saros menu. Enter the account handle of the second XMPP account we created, and press Finish. Soon we'll see a notification on the second computer (see Figure 31, *Prompt to confirm a new buddy*, on page 75).

Before we can connect to the buddy, however, we need to create a project to work on.

Figure 31—Prompt to confirm a new buddy

Sharing an Eclipse Project with Saros

To create an Eclipse project, select File -> New -> Project from the menu bar, and select General -> Project from the wizard that appears. Name it *myproject* and accept all the default settings.

Now we'll see myproject in the Package Explorer on the left side of Eclipse. Right-click this node, select New -> File, and choose the file readme.txt.

Now share this project by right-clicking on it again in the Package Explorer, select Share With, and then select the name of the buddy we added earlier, as shown in Figure 32, *Sharing an Eclipse project with a buddy*, on page 76. If you're working with only one computer, this step won't be possible.

Eclipse will prompt the buddy computer with an invitation to join the session. Once the invitation is accepted, the buddy will select a location to save the new project or synchronize with an existing project if this is not our first time sharing it. That's an important aspect of Saros because it means that both programmers will experience real-time write speed. There is no lag between pressing a key and seeing the change on our screen.

Because the two users are not sharing the same visual session (that is, each user has control of his own mouse, keyboard, and cursor), they can actually edit a document independently while the changes are synchronized in the background. Saros uses the Jupiter algorithm to resolve conflicts that occur during editing. It's the same algorithm Google uses in its Google Docs product line.

Once a project is shared, we have many options to choose from. We can grant or restrict read or write access to the buddy on a per-file basis. We can enter Follow Mode, which will follow our buddy's navigation through the IDE, or we can share our screen. This works out of the box on Windows but requires

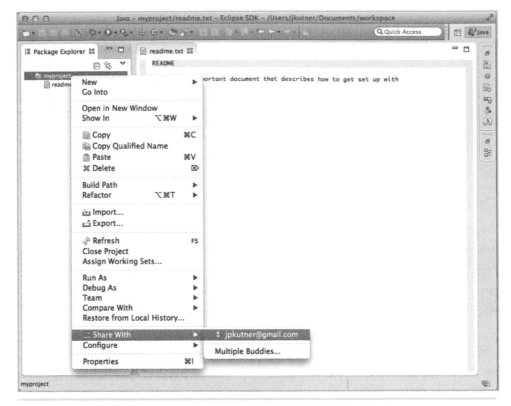

Figure 32—Sharing an Eclipse project with a buddy

some setup on other platforms. We'll also be notified of our buddy's activity by little yellow, green, and blue dots next to the icons of the files we're sharing.

Saros is a very robust collaborative editing environment. But it can do more than edit code.

Whiteboarding with Saros

One of the great features of Saros is that it enables graphical collaboration just as much as it enables textual collaboration. Take for example the Saros whiteboard, which creates a virtual brainstorming space to serve the purpose of a board in an office.

To open the whiteboard, select Window -> Show View from the menu bar. Then select Saros -> Saros Whiteboard from the Open View dialog. A toolbox pane will appear at the bottom of the Eclipse window; it's like the one in Figure 33, *Whiteboarding with Saros*, on page 77 except that ours will be empty. The tools include a pencil, basic shapes, lines, and text. These can be used to sketch out ideas as we collaborate with our pair-programming partner.

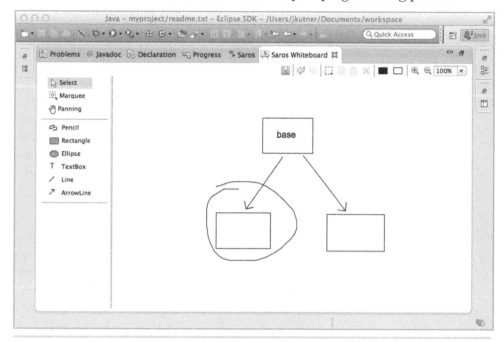

Figure 33—Whiteboarding with Saros

Because we're already sharing a session with a buddy, the whiteboard will also be shared. Try it out now. Draw some shapes and lines on the canvas, and watch as they appear on the second computer.

What's Next?

You've learned how to collaboratively edit source code with a pair-programming partner using a robust integrated development environment. That's great if you like the powerful features of an IDE and still want the collaborative features of tmux. It's also great when your connection is volatile—the conflict-resolution algorithm behind Saros ensures that you won't spend all of your time reconnecting. You can even continue to work if you go offline for a bit.

Saros is the most robust collaborative editing environment we could ask for. But you might find that an IDE like Eclipse is too heavy for your tastes —especially when you're working on smaller tasks. That's when any of the alternative IDE tools listed here might be a better solution:

Cloud9[4] This browser-based IDE supports real-time collaboration without installing any tools. It features syntax-coloring code completion, code folding, drag-and-drop, and many other standard IDE features.

Codenvy[5] A browser-based IDE that's similar to Cloud9. It supports customizable plug-ins that allow you to enhance its behavior. Additionally, it supports most major IDE features.

Gobby[6] A lightweight editor that provides real-time write speed, just like Saros. It synchronizes documents with the same Jupiter algorithm, and it provides unique features such as distinct cursors for each user. It has basic editing features like syntax coloring and tabs, but it's not nearly as configurable or extensible as Vim or Eclipse. As a result, it's rarely a first choice for remote pair programming. But it may be a handy tool when you need to do some quick editing of a small project.

Floobits[7] A Y Combinator–backed startup, Floobits's flagship offering is a pair-programming tool that leverages native text editors to collaborate on code in real time. The product supports Sublime Text, Vim, and Emacs. The software is a plug-in for the native editor. There's also a browser-based edition and a shell-sharing tool called Flooty.

SubEthaEdit[8] A text-editing program for Mac OS X. It uses the Bonjour protocol to connect users. It supports basic IDE-like features such as syntax coloring, code folding, and a command-line utility.

If you feel encumbered by the heavy hand of any IDE, you can always stick with the terminal-based stack we discussed in Chapter 2, *Collaborating with Text Only*, on page 11. The choice should be made between you and your pairing partner each time you start a session. Not every partner will want the same stack, which is why it's essential to equip yourself with an arsenal of remote pair programming tools. If your partner is located on the opposite side of the world, then Saros may suit you best. If your partner is sitting beside you but neither programmer wants to share a mouse and keyboard, then tmux may work great without sharing screens.

In the next chapter, we'll take a look at how the technologies you've learned about are used in the real world.

---

4. https://c9.io/
5. https://codenvy.com/
6. http://gobby.0x539.de/
7. https://floobits.com/
8. http://www.subethaedit.de/

CHAPTER 7

Remote Pairing in the Wild

Most programmers have suffered from Impostor Syndrome at some point in their career. Impostor Syndrome is characterized by self-doubt and feelings of inadequacy that overshadow personal success and accomplishments. For some reason, programmers are particularly prone to this trait, and pairing sessions sometimes make it worse by putting your programming skills to the test in front of another person. But pairing isn't a test, and with the right etiquette, methods, and courtesies, it won't feel that way. In this chapter, we'll explore common guidelines that help relieve the pressures of pairing. We'll examine case studies of real teams that pair remotely every day, and you'll learn how they deal with the human element when working with another person.

Pair programming can act as an antidote for Impostor Syndrome by providing external validation of your abilities and bolstering your confidence. You'll still make occasional mistakes in your sessions, but you'll learn that other programmers make mistakes, too. These mistakes should be thought of as learning experiences. Through them, you and your partner will acquire new abilities and techniques that improve your productivity. Let's meet a few programmers who know this firsthand.

Pairing at Test Double

Test Double is a software consultancy specializing in front-end web development.[1] The company doesn't have a central office where its employees meet (at least for now), and its clients are located throughout the United States. The distributed structure of the company is by design, and the founders leverage this to gain flexibility in who they hire and what customers they work with.

---

1. http://testdouble.com/

As a result, developers at Test Double do a lot of remote pair programming and often coach clients who are new to pairing. But even these experts had to start somewhere.

"When I was first getting used to pairing...I behaved differently," says Test Double cofounder Justin Searls. "I [was] out of my element. I wouldn't use as many declarative statements, and I'd ask a lot of questions." Justin's confidence grew after many years of colocated and remote pairing, and he became more comfortable—especially in the areas of technology he'd mastered. "I can dive in...and shape the experience," he says. "So the other person learns the right habits."

Justin likes to be a good influence on his pairing partners, but he doesn't try to overpower them. In fact, he believes it's better when partners come together as peers. "There are lots of right ways to do things," he believes. "It's less important that we pick your way or my way, and it's more important that we normalize on an approach and focus on the hard problems that actually matter." Often, that means both programmers have to make compromises.

"For me, pairing is all about being vulnerable enough and aware enough to merge with another person," Justin explains. And he's found that merging as peers is particularly important when projects are at their most difficult point. He encourages developers to be honest and forthcoming about what they know, what they don't know, and when they see things that are potentially dangerous. "Whether it's remote or in person—at the outset of a project, when things are risky, or there are a lot of unknowns...that's when pairing is most valuable." And that's also when you start learning new techniques.

There are two predominant camps of developers at Test Double: those who use Vim and those who use Sublime Text,[2] a lightweight, graphical-based code editor with some powerful features. When two Vim users pair together, the technology stack is similar to the tmux, SSH, and Vim environment we built in Chapter 2, *Collaborating with Text Only*, on page 11, and Chapter 3, *Using the Cloud to Connect*, on page 27. But when a Vim user pairs with a Sublime user, the Vim user usually has to give up these terminal-based tools.

Sublime Text lacks a built-in pairing mechanism and it can't be shared over tmux. That leaves screen sharing as the only means of collaboration. The preferred screen-sharing tools at Test Double are VNC-based applications like the ones discussed in Chapter 4, *Collaborating with Shared Screens*, on page 43, as well as some commercial products.

---

2. http://www.sublimetext.com/

"The most popular is TeamViewer," says Justin. "We all hate TeamViewer, but it's cross-platform and faster than VNC." TeamViewer is a software package that targets remote administration and online meetings more than pair programming,[3] but many paired teams prefer it. Justin found that by tweaking some settings, such as turning off color, he's able to decrease latency and reduce the eye fatigue resulting from occasional lag and flickering when sharing screens. Customizations that improve the connection speed are important because bandwidth is the most critical problem Justin faces when remote-pairing.

"Bandwidth is a big problem for anyone who's trying to accomplish this in a home-to-home setting," Justin shares. "If I'm using a VNC-based tool and scrolling through a page, which means lots of pixels are getting refreshed, suddenly people can't hear me or my sentences start breaking up." It hasn't stopped Justin or any of the developers at Test Double from remote-pairing, but they occasionally have to work around these issues—especially when they work from low-bandwidth environments. "Sometimes I want to work at a coffee shop with other humans," says Justin, "and I have to plan my day around that. I have to pull off a chunk of work that I can do independently before I go out." But the tmux and Vim developers don't have this problem as long as they aren't sharing a screen. Justin says, "The Vimmers love pairing with each other."

Despite having two technology stacks at Test Double, the team is able to function well because every programmer has some level of proficiency with each environment. And many of the developers learned the secondary technology stack by pairing with someone who already mastered it. Sharing knowledge, however, is possible only when both parties are actively engaged in the pairing session. Justin occasionally has to remind himself of this fact. "I catch myself...reading something else, distracting myself on other stuff, and maybe even tricking myself into thinking I'm multitasking," he admits. "[When that happens] I have to rein it in, and take a formal break."

The need to enforce his own good behavior led Justin to make an unusual technology choice. "I have more success when I'm on my 11-inch MacBook," he says. "I have to full-screen [my code], and I'm not tempted to go click on another window."

Justin has learned how to recognize many cues, like becoming distracted, that tell him it might be time to change things up. "Once it's boring to pair with somebody, or I know exactly what [my partner] is going to type before

---

3.   http://www.teamviewer.com/en/index.aspx

[he] types it, that's when I stop pairing." Justin says. "Once it gets boring, then we can have two lines of work."

For a novice, it may be difficult to tell when it's time to stop pairing. But maybe you don't need to stop. Many expert pair programmers do it all day, every day.

Pairing at Pivotal Labs

Pivotal Labs is a software firm based in San Francisco.[4] You may be familiar with its flagship product, Pivotal Tracker,[5] but the company does a wide range of other software development—client work, iPhone apps, and more.

Pivotal uses a strict system of pair programming, in which most developers pair with another developer every time they sit down to write code. That's eight hours a day, five days a week. The majority of Pivotal's employees work in one of the company's seven major offices, but a handful of developers work from remote locations. Despite the distance, these anywhere-based developers adhere to the same strict pairing policy.

One of Pivotal's veteran remote developers is Joe Moore, who's become an outspoken advocate for remote pair programming. His blog is an excellent source for pairing-technology news, and he's given a number of public talks on the subject.[6,7] Joe started as an on-site Pivotal employee, but moved out of the office in 2010 so his wife could continue her medical career. Despite his change of location, things at Pivotal remained largely the same.

Joe's morning starts with a stand-up meeting where he and his team decide who will pair with who that day. "We try to swap pairs every day if we can," he says. "If we can't, we try to monitor people who have paired together too many days in a row [because] it's usually an indication that they're stuck on something."

Given Joe's many partners, his stack of software tools varies significantly from day to day. "It depends on the logistics of the client, network speed, security, and VPN," he says. Most of the time, Joe can rely on tmux and Vim, but since he's primarily a web developer he usually needs a screen-sharing tool to supplement his text editor. He prefers either Screenhero or the built-in Mac Screen Sharing app we discussed in Chapter 4, *Collaborating with*

---

4.   http://pivotallabs.com/
5.   https://www.pivotaltracker.com/
6.   http://remotepairprogramming.com/
7.   http://remotepairprogramming.com/tagged/video

Shared Screens, on page 43.[8] These software tools are significant, but they aren't as important to Joe as the human element. "I find that [video] is invaluable," he says. "I want to be able to see people's faces. I want to know if they're confused, if they're laughing, or if they're looking down at their phone." His preference has led to a very elaborate home-office setup. Joe has multiple monitors and a retractable arm that holds an iPad for running his Skype sessions. "It looks like Fort Knox or something," he muses.

Video is important because it allows Joe to quickly pick up on subtle cues that might otherwise be missed. But sometimes there's just no replacement for telling your partner what you're thinking. "I can't see your hands and you can't see my hands, so all day long I'm saying things like, 'Hey, I'm going to grab the mouse' or, 'Do you mind if I look at something?' instead of just doing it," he explains. "I replace a lot of [visual cues] with verbal cues." Joe believes that verbalizing everything leads to better pairing etiquette. Many of his on-site pairing partners say that learning to do this has helped improve their colocated pair sessions, too.

Joe has been able to use video and verbal cues to keep his pairing sessions extremely fluid. He's found that the advantage of having more than one person working on a problem is that you have more ideas, which makes it easier to overcome obstacles. "There's so much shared experience [that] there's seldom a time when we're truly stuck," he says. "Once you get down to it...it stops being novel and just becomes the way you work."

Joe loves pairing with his Pivotal team, and he finds that doing eight hours a day works perfectly for him. But he acknowledges that a routine of 100 percent pairing might not be perfect for everyone: "Some people don't have a good setup at home. Maybe they don't feel comfortable or there are too many distractions, but some pairing is better than none." For some teams, the best time to get that little bit of daily remote pairing is when they're having problems.

Pairing at Big Nerd Ranch

Big Nerd Ranch, an industry leader in iOS development and training,[9] doesn't have a strict policy of pairing like Pivotal Labs. Instead, developers decide on their own when pairing is appropriate. Jay Hayes, a programmer at Big Nerd Ranch, says this leads to an informal remote-pairing environment. Jay lives in Alabama, 200 miles away from the company headquarters in Atlanta. Most

---

8. http://screenhero.com/
9. http://www.bignerdranch.com

of his team members are based in Atlanta, but none of them are required to make regular trips to the office. Despite the distance, they still manage to pair up on tough problems.

"It doesn't usually start with 'Hey, why don't we pair a bit when you have some downtime,'" says Jay. "It's more like 'I've been banging my head against the desk, and can anyone help me crush this bug?'" Jay believes this ad hoc approach helps his team function more like a colocated one. "Our pairing ends up being just like if you were in the office and needed help. Someone might come over and sit with you for a bit—it's a remote version of that," he feels. Despite using an "as needed" approach to pairing, Jay does it about once a day—but the sessions don't often last long: "Maybe thirty minutes on average...and we don't use any formal methods."

Jay's preferred tech stack is tmux and Vim, which he uses for both pairing and working solo. The team uses Google Hangouts to share screens, but they occasionally resort to using Screenhero when they need two-way control, a browser, or an integrated development environment.

Jay is pretty handy with Vim, but that wasn't always the case. Upon joining Big Nerd Ranch, he knew how to open Vim, exit Vim, move up and down, and nothing else. "[Learning Vim] was top priority on my list," Jay reveals. "It was amazing.... I paired with people, and within two days I was exclusively in Vim." He attributes his dramatic conversion to simple observation. "I could quickly absorb the little tips and tricks just by watching. Anytime I was pairing with someone using Vim I'd ask, 'Hey, how did you do that?'" After a while, Jay found that he was teaching other programmers some of his own tricks. He proclaims, "The best way to learn stuff is to do it with other people."

Jay's giant steps toward mastering Vim are a great example of why it's important to check your ego at the door and never be afraid to ask questions when pairing. "I went in with a very practical understanding of my ability," he says. "I expected to be overwhelmed...but I was very surprised at how much I already knew."

Ad hoc pairing is working for Jay's team, but he still tries to introduce more structure when he can. "I like the idea of officially establishing the driver and navigator in each session," he explains, "but we don't usually do that." The idea of having specific roles originated with colocated pair programming, and corresponds to various patterns often used to delegate responsibilities and keep a session's momentum going. Although some of these are popular, they are equally despised by some teams.

Patterns of Pairing

In the early days of extreme programming, a number of patterns emerged that served to coordinate how two developers worked together. They probably came about because the concept of pairing was new, and most programmers weren't used to anything other than working alone. Some of these patterns deal with issues specific to colocated pairs, but a few have carried over into remote pairing.

Tag Team   In this pattern, programmers take turns as the *driver*, who is in control of the keyboard, and the *navigator*, who contributes to the task verbally. The pair can alternate between these roles at preset time intervals or in an ad hoc fashion. In both cases, the driver writes code while the navigator acts as a reviewer and/or foreman. As reviewer, the navigator is responsible for identifying any mistakes the driver makes at the code level. As foreman, the navigator is responsible for thinking strategically about the overall structure of the code base and whether the code is solving the business problem at hand.[10]

Ping-Pong   This pattern is an extension of both the tag-team pattern and test-driven development. The process begins with a programmer writing a test to define some new behavior or replicate a bug. The test will fail because it's new, at which point the first programmer passes control to the second programmer, whose job is to make the test pass. Throughout the process, both programmers communicate and discuss the problem, but control of the mouse and keyboard is strictly divided between the two phases.

Let the Junior Drive   This pattern assumes one programmer is a novice and the other programmer is significantly more experienced. For the entire session, the more experienced programmer acts as the navigator while the less experienced programmer acts as the driver. It's important to note that some experts consider this an antipattern, as it can slow down the session by restricting fluid interaction between programmers. That might explain why studies conducted on real pairing sessions at large-scale companies find the boundaries between these roles break down in practice —resulting to an approach more similar to tag team than anything else.[11]

Parallel Pairing (aka Buddy Programming)   In this pattern, two programmers work independently on the same problem and converge at the end to compare solutions and ultimately merge them. In this way, it mimics the

---

10. *Pair Programming Illuminated [WK02]*
11. *Pair programming and the mysterious role of the navigator [BRd08]*

difference between concurrency and parallelism in computer systems. Parallel pairing is not truly pairing, but it does have the advantage of eliminating many of the technical challenges described in this book because developers work independently for the most part.

Trio Programming   This includes any scenario in which more than two programmers attempt to work together on the same piece of code. Most of the tools discussed in this book, including tmux and VNC, support sharing with multiple users. In both cases, the host starts a session as normal while multiple clients connect to the session from distinct machines. As with the tag-team pattern, only one person acts as the driver during the session, but there will be multiple navigators. Thus, it's important to clearly define each person's role when implementing this pattern. Trio programming is often used when pair programming is strictly enforced (that is, solo programming is forbidden) but the team has an odd number of members. The disadvantage of this pattern is that each programmer gets less time to drive than would be the case with fewer people in the session. For this reason, many organizations discourage it. Joe Moore calls it an antipattern.

By most accounts, experienced pair programmers don't use these patterns—at least intentionally. The programmers at Test Double, Pivotal Labs, Big Nerd Ranch, and several other companies describe a typical pair-programming session as being largely unstructured. If they follow any pattern, it might best be described as an ad hoc tag-team pattern. These programmers are experienced enough at pairing that they don't need the rigidity of strict patterns. But there are a some exceptions.

"Ping-pong is great in interviews [and] in coaching situations," says Justin Searls. "In an environment where [no one] has done pairing before...[I'm] a little more formal and I start with ping-pong so that people have good prompts for what's next."

As you remote-pair-program, begin to use the ping-pong pattern. It will give you and your partner clear cues that help you learn when to switch roles. As you become more comfortable, move on to the tag-team pattern with preset intervals. Switch to the ad hoc tag-team pattern only when you begin to feel that you can comfortably anticipate the need to switch roles. You may end up loving or hating these patterns, but in either case you'll learn more about what works and what doesn't when pairing remotely. After time, you'll develop your own methods and patterns that work for you and your organization.

Wrapping Up

The majority of this book focuses on solving technical problems, but some of the most difficult remote-pairing issues are people problems. If you follow the advice of the programmers in this chapter you'll be well on your way to solving or even avoiding them entirely. But sometimes technology can solve people problems, too. Your software stack can improve cooperation and make the remote-pairing experience smooth and comfortable. If you're happy with your tools, you'll probably be more productive.

Whatever tools you choose, remember that a human being sits at the other end of the connection. The same rules of etiquette that apply to colocated pair programming apply to remote pair programming. In fact, communication, sharing, and listening to your partner might be *more* important when pairing remotely.

Go pair with someone right now. Pick a project you know nothing about—try the Linux kernel.[12] Then grab a friend or post a tweet on Twitter with the #pairwithme hash tag. You can say something as simple as, "I want to learn about the Linux kernel. Anyone want to #pairwithme?" It's almost guaranteed that in the following thirty minutes you'll learn something new that improves your daily programming routine.

---

12. https://github.com/torvalds/linux

Bibliography

[ABB98]   A. Anderson, R. Beattie, and K. Beck. Chrysler Goes to 'Extremes'. *Distributed Computing*. 1998.

[BGS02]   Prashant Baheti, Edward F. Gehringer, and P. David Stotts. Exploring the efficacy of distributed pair programming. *Proceedings of the Second XP Universe and First Agile Universe Conference on Extreme Programming and Agile Methods*. 2418, 2002.

[BOLR10]   Bahador Bahrami, Karsten Olsen, Peter E. Latham, Andreas Roepstorff, Geraint Rees, and Chris D. Frith. Optimally Interacting Minds. *Science*. 329[5995], 2010.

[BRd08]   Sallyann Bryant, Pablo Romero, and Benedict du Boulay. Pair programming and the mysterious role of the navigator. *International Journal of Human-Computer Studies*. 66[7], 2008.

[CW00]   Alistair Cockburn and Laurie Williams. The costs and benefits of pair programming. *Extreme Programming Examined*. 2000.

[DL99]   Tom Demarco and Timothy Lister. *Peopleware: Productive Projects and Teams*. Dorset House, New York, NY, USA, Second, 1999.

[HDAS09]   Jo E. Hannay, Tore Dybå, Erik Arisholm, and Dag I.K. Sjøberg. The Effectiveness of Pair Programming: A Meta-Analysis. *Information and Software Technology*. 51[7], 2009.

[Han02]   Brian Hanks. Empirical evaluation of distributed pair programming. *International Journal of Human-Computer Studies*. 66[7], 2002.

[Hog12]   Brian P. Hogan. *tmux: Productive Mouse-Free Development*. The Pragmatic Bookshelf, Raleigh, NC and Dallas, TX, 2012.

[LO11]   Jeff Langr and Tim Ottinger. *Agile in a Flash: Speed-Learning Agile Software Development*. The Pragmatic Bookshelf, Raleigh, NC and Dallas, TX, 2011.

[Nos98]   John T. Nosek. The case for collaborative programming. *Communications of the ACM.* 41[3], 1998.

[VCK96]   John Vlissides, James O. Coplien, and Norman L. Kerth. *Pattern Languages of Program Design 2.* Addison-Wesley, Reading, MA, 1996.

[WK02]   Laurie Williams and Robert Kessler. *Pair Programming Illuminated.* Addison-Wesley, Reading, MA, 2002.

[WKCJ00]   Laurie Williams, Robert R. Kessler, Ward Cunningham, and Ron Jeffries. Strengthening the case for pair programming. *Software.* 17[4], 2000.

Healthy Programming and The Joy of Math

Rediscover the joy and fascinating weirdness of pure mathematics, and learn how to take a healthier approach to programming.

The Healthy Programmer

To keep doing what you love, you need to maintain your own systems, not just the ones you write code for. Regular exercise and proper nutrition help you learn, remember, concentrate, and be creative—skills critical to doing your job well. Learn how to change your work habits, master exercises that make working at a computer more comfortable, and develop a plan to keep fit, healthy, and sharp for years to come.

This book is intended only as an informative guide for those wishing to know more about health issues. In no way is this book intended to replace, countermand, or conflict with the advice given to you by your own healthcare provider including Physician, Nurse Practitioner, Physician Assistant, Registered Dietician, and other licensed professionals.

Joe Kutner
(254 pages) ISBN: 9781937785314. $36
http://pragprog.com/book/jkthp

Good Math

Mathematics is beautiful—and it can be fun and exciting as well as practical. *Good Math* is your guide to some of the most intriguing topics from two thousand years of mathematics: from Egyptian fractions to Turing machines; from the real meaning of numbers to proof trees, group symmetry, and mechanical computation. If you've ever wondered what lay beyond the proofs you struggled to complete in high school geometry, or what limits the capabilities of the computer on your desk, this is the book for you.

Mark C. Chu-Carroll
(282 pages) ISBN: 9781937785338. $34
http://pragprog.com/book/mcmath

The Pragmatic Bookshelf

The Pragmatic Bookshelf features books written by developers for developers. The titles continue the well-known Pragmatic Programmer style and continue to garner awards and rave reviews. As development gets more and more difficult, the Pragmatic Programmers will be there with more titles and products to help you stay on top of your game.

Visit Us Online

This Book's Home Page
http://pragprog.com/book/jkrp
Source code from this book, errata, and other resources. Come give us feedback, too!

Register for Updates
http://pragprog.com/updates
Be notified when updates and new books become available.

Join the Community
http://pragprog.com/community
Read our weblogs, join our online discussions, participate in our mailing list, interact with our wiki, and benefit from the experience of other Pragmatic Programmers.

New and Noteworthy
http://pragprog.com/news
Check out the latest pragmatic developments, new titles and other offerings.

Save on the eBook

Save on the eBook versions of this title. Owning the paper version of this book entitles you to purchase the electronic versions at a terrific discount.

PDFs are great for carrying around on your laptop—they are hyperlinked, have color, and are fully searchable. Most titles are also available for the iPhone and iPod touch, Amazon Kindle, and other popular e-book readers.

Buy now at *http://pragprog.com/coupon*

Contact Us

Online Orders:	*http://pragprog.com/catalog*
Customer Service:	*support@pragprog.com*
International Rights:	*translations@pragprog.com*
Academic Use:	*academic@pragprog.com*
Write for Us:	*http://pragprog.com/write-for-us*
Or Call:	+1 800-699-7764

CPSIA information can be obtained at www.ICGtesting.com
Printed in the USA
LVOW03s0202080114

368466LV00019B/103/P